If you're a member of the human race, chances are that one of these days you'll be giving a speech.

Maybe you've never given a speech. Maybe you're terrified. But you do realize it's possible to learn to stand before a group and speak to them.

Maybe you're an experienced speaker—a salesperson, manager, supervisor, or board member. But it's been a while since you've studied public speaking. Now a refresher course might help.

Whoever you are, whatever your experience, you *can* learn how to overcome stage fright—in eight steps. Don't be kidded into thinking they are easy. But they are platform-tested, clear, and specific. Most important—they work!

Here's the book that will teach you . . .

HOW TO
SPEAK LIKE
A PRO!

HOW TO

SPEAK LIKE

A PRO

Leon Fletcher

BALLANTINE BOOKS • NEW YORK

PN
4121
.F6
1988
147456
Oct.1989

Library of Congress Catalog Card Number: 82-90864

ISBN 0-345-33427-2

Printed in Canada

First Edition: March 1983
Ninth Printing: September 1988

TO MY WIFE, VIVIAN

CONTENTS

INTRODUCTION

Why should you learn to "speak like a pro?"

I've found, during my quarter-century in management, that most successful people have one thing in common: They can speak. They can verbalize their ideas so that those ideas are heard, understood, and acted upon.

As modern society becomes increasingly complex, there is an ever-expanding need for effective verbal communication. Never before has it been more vital for men and women to transmit verbal messages that inform, persuade, entertain, motivate, and inspire. By developing this ability, you will arm yourself with the greatest success and leadership tool you can have.

No one is more qualified to write a book like this than my good friend Leon Fletcher. Leon is a distinguished educator and author whose knowledge and experience are unsurpassed. He also has the ability to write in a clear, crisp manner that makes learning easy.

If you seek to become an effective public speaker, I urge you to do two things:

First, read this excellent book. Let Leon Fletcher show you what it takes to construct and deliver a good speech.

Then, get on your feet and speak. As good as this book is, it can't make you a good speaker unless you put its principles to work.

Don't worry if you don't "speak like a pro" on your first few attempts. Stay with it, and before long you'll have developed a skill that can truly change your life.

Good speaking,

Terrence J. McCann,
Executive Director,
Toastmasters International

1

Speaking Up!

> *Let thy speech be better than
> silence, or be silent.*
>
> DIONYSIUS

MORE PEOPLE SEEM to be giving more speeches than ever before.

No one is keeping score, but the increase in public speaking seems clear, dramatic, and widespread.

Business people are speaking at conferences, seminars, workshops. Parents are pleading to school boards for better schools. Ecologists are giving speeches to help preserve our lands. Housewives are speaking out about women's issues. Politicians are appealing for votes. The elderly and retired give talks about their unique problems. Minorities are becoming more vocal about their needs, their goals, their frustrations.

Most of us spend about seven out of every ten waking hours communicating. Three-fourths of our communication is by speech.

The result: The average person speaks some 34,020 words a day. That's equal to several books a week, more than twelve million words a year.

Speech is "essential" to some seven of every ten jobs says the Department of Labor. Off the job, speech is even more important.

You may well be asked, or assigned, or you may volunteer to give a speech. It may be a talk related to your job, or it may be for some social, hobby, organization, or other activity.

But few of us like to stand up and talk before an audience. We're nervous. We worry about saying something wrong. We're afraid we won't sound good. Or look all right. We're concerned that people might not listen. Or maybe they won't believe us. Maybe they won't remember what we say.

And it seems like it's an awful lot of work to get ready to give a speech. Worst of all, just the thought of giving a speech makes us nervous!

All those concerns are valid. Professional speakers as well as beginners face them.

This book will help you overcome those problems. It will show you—step-by-step—how to plan and then present effective speeches. You'll learn how to control your nerves, pinpoint your subject, find information, organize and practice your speech. You'll become skilled in answering questions, using a microphone, introducing a speaker, and much, much more.

But many people wonder—"Is public speaking all that useful today?"

It is indeed!

* Citizens are speaking up much more frequently to government agencies. People just like you—along with many others who are far less intelligent or educated—are presenting their ideas to city councils, school boards, county trustees, planning commissions, state committees, federal hearings, to public meetings of all kinds.
* Businesses and industries are holding more and more meetings for sales staffs, production teams, management personnel, all levels and all kinds of employees. They give speeches about safety and success, cooperation and competition, production and personality, motivation and meditation and a mind-boggling range of other topics.
* Clubs, associations, and other organizations are having more and more of their members take part in meetings. In many groups, the president, chair-

man, or leader is asking or telling someone else to talk about the next project, to brief new members, or to summarize last week's board meeting.

* Churches are getting their members to present parts of the services and to speak more frequently at other activities.

* Participants in self-help and self-study groups give talks to each other. Their subjects range from planning for their financial future to finding out about their previous lives on this earth.

* *Toastmasters,* the international club in which members help each other become better speakers, has nearly doubled its membership in the last five years.

* Across the nation, more than sixty-five cities have built conference centers with special rooms and equipment for public speakers.

* More than 26,000,000 Americans go to over 250,000 conferences each year, where more speeches are given than anyone has counted.

But why might *you* have to give a speech?

* Your company sent you to a conference and upon your return, management wants you to brief other staff members about what you learned.

* You've had it with tax increases! You decide you just have to go to a meeting of your city council and plead with them to cut down on all the projects they're approving.

* You're a member of a service club or a fraternal organization and you've been asked to announce a new proposal.

* You're active in your local environmental group and you want to get others involved.

* You're a volunteer teacher's aide at your child's school and have to give talks to the students now and then.

* You're coaching a little league team or counseling a youth group, giving pep talks, suggesting plans, reporting to the sponsors.

* You have a friend running for an elective office and he expects you to speak for him at the next meeting of your club.
* You've been called to serve on the funding committee at your church, to present an appeal for funds to various groups within the congregation.

If you're a member of the human race, chances are high that one of these days you'll be giving a speech.

You may be an experienced speaker—salesperson, manager, supervisor, teacher, board member, or such. But it's been awhile since you've had a course in public speaking. Now a refresher, a reinforcement of your speaking skills plus a review of what's new in how to give a talk, might help.

Or maybe you've never given a speech, never studied how. But you can see that it is certainly possible that before long you, too, will be standing before an audience, giving a speech.

Here's how—in eight steps. You won't be kidded into thinking these are easy steps. But they are platform-tested, clear, and specific. Most important—they work! They can indeed help *you* to speak like a pro!

2

Why Pros Are Successful

> Speech was made to open
> man to man, and not to hide
> him; to promote commerce,
> and not betray it.
>
> DAVID LLOYD

ALMOST ALL SUCCESSFUL professional speakers follow these two basic principles:

#1: They don't try to talk like someone else.
#2: They don't give a speech without preparing.

Here is how you can use those principles so you'll be an effective speaker.

First, like the professional, you shouldn't try to sound like anyone other than yourself. More than 400 years ago Shakespeare had Polonius tell Hamlet, "To thine own self be true." That's still good advice for every speaker.

Don't try to talk like that popular teacher who had all the kids waiting in line to sign up for his classes. Don't think you have to imitate that inspirational minister you heard at church. Don't dream of copying that guy with a gift of gab, or that gal who is a TV reporter.

Besides, the typical meek, mild, modest speaker doesn't really have much of a chance of turning into a

powerful, dramatic, exciting orator. But then, there's no real reason for you to change your own personality, your own way of talking. *You certainly can be a successful speaker without trying to change yourself into a golden-voiced orator.*

Furthermore, orators—those formal, dignified, booming speakers—are not the typical successful speakers of today.

Today most effective speakers talk in conversational tones. They are informal. Personable. Today, most good speakers talk *with*—not at—their listeners.

If you're giving a speech to a small group of people —say up to around forty or so listeners—you can probably be heard without using a public address system. You may have to speak a bit louder, but your general tone can remain pretty much as if you were talking in an informal conversation with a few friends.

If you're speaking to a large audience, in a hall or an auditorium, modern electronic aids let you speak with that same personalized delivery. Modern microphones and good sound systems can carry your voice to hundreds of people and make them feel as if you're speaking with them as individuals.

On television and radio, with audiences often running into the millions, many of the most effective speakers talk in casual, conversational styles. They realize they're not addressing gigantic audiences. They're really talking with people individually or in small groups of just two or three or so people. Usually we watch TV while sitting around at home—informally. We listen to the radio at home, too, or we may listen in our car, as we drive alone, or with just one or a few others. The best of many of today's speakers capitalize on those casual settings by talking with us in a natural, calm style.

Sure, some golden-voiced spellbinders are still around. They'll shout at their listeners one moment, then drop their voices to a whisper. Some TV evangelists deliver their pleas in dramatic, soul-stirring tones.

But often such appeals produce just short-term effects. Telethons in which speakers are overly emotional in pleading for contributions often collect far less than is

pledged. Many of those people who step forward to the speaker's platform to make a spiritual commitment at a religious crusade don't follow through by joining a church.

In almost all speaking situations, it's the speaker who talks in his or her own personal, natural, conversational style who is most effective. Be yourself and you are more likely to get your ideas across, deliver information, stimulate action.

Of course, you may already be one of those people who can give a speech with the drama of a Billy Graham, a Dick Gregory, a Paul Harvey, or a Helen Hayes. Then you should certainly use your skill. Speak in a style which makes you comfortable.

That, then, is the first principle followed by the successful professional speaker—don't try to sound like anyone other than yourself.

The second principle of the successful pro, you'll remember, is don't give a speech without preparing. You can prepare effectively and efficiently for your speeches by following these eight steps:

Step #1: Control Your Stage Fright
Step #2: Select Your Subject
Step #3: Gather Your Ideas and Information
Step #4: Organize Your Material
Step #5: Plan the Beginning of Your Speech
Step #6: Plan the Ending of Your Speech
Step #7: Practice Your Speech
Step #8: Present Your Speech

Exactly how to complete each of those steps is presented in the next chapters.

One caution. You probably won't get very far into those steps before you start thinking, *Wait a minute! I haven't heard many speakers use many of these techniques!!*

And you'll be right. Few speakers do plan and present their speeches in the form and style detailed in this book. But of all the speeches you've heard, HOW MANY DO YOU REMEMBER?

If you're like most of us, you remember very, very little of what a speaker says. Studies show that the average person remembers only about twenty-five percent of what he hears. And he remembers that little bit for but a short time. After forty-eight hours, most of us can recall only about ten percent of what we really tried to remember from a speech. When we listen to the typical public speaker—especially to a speech we may not have any real need or desire to remember—we often recall even less.

The reason we don't remember most of what we hear in speeches is not necessarily that we listen poorly or that we have faulty memories. Rather, it's often because so few speakers use effective speaking techniques.

We hear some politician give a speech and a couple of hours later we may meet a friend who says, "I missed that speech. What did he say?" And we're stuck! Often, all we can remember is the general idea of the speech. We'll answer, "Well, he said he was against higher taxes." "Great! What's he going to do to stop them?" Now we really have to dig through our memory banks. But we find little—or nothing—there. The speaker didn't present his ideas in specific terms. He didn't state them in a logical order. He simply failed to make his speech memorable.

The techniques and tips presented in this book are platform-tested. They are basically the same methods good speakers have been using for centuries. The successful communicators of centuries ago, way back to the days of Cicero, Aristotle, Sophocles, and others, used and urged others to use many of these techniques. Yet the most modern and successful of today's public speakers continue to use essentially the same basic methods to prepare and present their speeches. Here you'll be reading examples from speakers ranging from Johnny Carson to President Reagan, from Joan Rivers to Barbara Walters. Throughout the ages, **preparation** has been a basic key to successful speaking.

3

STEP #1: Control Your Stage Fright

> *The human brain is a wonderful thing. It operates from the moment you're born until the first time you get up to make a speech.*
>
> HOWARD GOSHORN

FOR MOST OF US, the prospect of giving a speech is enough to make us nervous.

Our hands may sweat. Our eyes may blur. The mouth goes dry.

Usually, all that discomfort disappears quickly. After all, you don't have to speak for a couple of weeks. You relax. For a while.

As the time for your speech draws near, nervousness often returns. Your stomach seems to flutter. Breathing becomes faster. Your voice cracks. Words—even simple words—are hard to get out.

You know the cause: stage fright. Actors call it "flop sweat." Psychologists call it "topophobia."

"Don't soften it with those gentle words," one speaker told me. "PANIC!!!—that's what it is!"

Whatever you call it, stage fright is the one problem faced by virtually every speaker—beginner and professional. Recently 3,000 Americans were asked, "What are you most afraid of?" Their most frequent reply:

"Speaking before a group." It was named more often than financial problems, illness, even death.

Controlling stage fright is the first step in this program of speech preparation because it's a problem for almost every speaker. We stay awake nights, worrying about a speech we have to give. We try to think through what we'll say and the mind goes blank!

But stage fright can be controlled. *You* can control it! While few speakers are able to eliminate it, almost everyone can reduce it, adjust to it, speak effectively in spite of it. Indeed, many professionals claim they speak effectively—at least in part—*because* of stage fright. Actor Carroll O'Connor of the TV shows *All in the Family* and *Archie's Place* said this about stage fright:

> A professional actor has a kind of tension. The amateur is thrown by it but the professional needs it.

You can develop the professional's control of stage fright through SEVEN SPECIFIC STEPS.

1. *Recognize that you are not alone in suffering from stage fright.*

Start right at the top—the Presidents of the United States.

* President Reagan reveals his nervousness while speaking by dipping his head, grinning, starting many sentences with "Well! . . ."
* Carter clasped his hands together, fingers intertwined so tightly his knuckles turned white.
* Ford pursed his lips, gestured gracelessly, fumbled one-syllable words.
* Nixon, since his earliest days as a college debater, suffered stage fright which made sweat pour down his face.
* Johnson repeated "ah's," struggled for words, filled his speeches with long pauses.

* Kennedy clawed the air with his index finger, searching for a word or idea.
* Eisenhower's nervousness produced sentences so complex many English teachers could neither diagram nor understand them.
* Truman showed his stage fright through one almost continuous gesture—moving both hands up and down in unison.

Then there are the stars of show business, suffering from nerves just like you and me.

* Jimmy Stewart, quoted in *Time* magazine: 'I've never been able to overcome the fear thing.'
* Ethel Merman on a TV talk show: 'I cannot give a speech—I'm petrified!'
* Carol Burnett: 'The idea of making a speech does more than make me a nervous wreck; it terrifies me!'

TV hosts Johnny Carson, Merv Griffin, Dinah Shore, Jack Paar, Peter Marshall have all talked about their nervousness on camera. So have such diverse personalities as Henry Winkler, Robert Alda, Liza Minnelli, Sally Struthers, Orson Welles, George Gobel, Paul Lynde, Sidney Poitier, Erica Jong, Dick Van Patten, Joan Rivers, Jack Klugman, McLean Stevenson, Christopher Reeves, Maureen Stapleton, and more. *Many* more!

You've got stage fright? You are *not* alone!

But even more important is this fact:

2. *We all appear much more confident than we feel.*

To check out the truth of that statement, ask a friend how you look and sound as you practice a speech, or as you give a speech in a real situation. Or, make a tape recording of yourself as you speak or practice.

But to really prove to yourself that you do indeed look much more confident than you feel, watch a videotape recording of yourself. Today, that's a lot easier to do than you may think.

You don't have to apply for a spot on the *Johnny Carson Show*. Instead, visit your local university, college, elementary or high school, where many instructional television systems are now used. Or check with your friends—a growing number of people have their own private, home-TV recording systems.

Such systems do not "broadcast"—they don't send the TV picture out on the air. They can't be picked up on another TV receiver. Rather, these are "closed-circuit systems"—the camera, recorder, and viewing set are simply tied together with direct wiring. The tapes on which your picture and voice are recorded can be erased and reused.

Seeing yourself on such a system should prove to you that you do, indeed, look and sound much more calm, confident, polished than you may feel. If you'll look at yourself on TV with just a bit of honesty, you'll have to admit that while you may not be another Barbara Walters or Tom Brokaw, still you certainly are not really very different from them.

All you need to record is a brief statement—just a minute or two of your speaking in your own style. You might use part of a speech you've already given, one you're planning, a summary of a story you read in the morning paper, a brief description of your hobby or a recent trip.

When you watch the tape being played back, ignore those details that most people concentrate on the first time they see themselves on TV. Forget the tie that may be crooked, the ruffled blouse, the lipstick that's too dark, the hair out of place. Instead, focus on *what* you say and *how* you say it.

Have the recording played back for you two or three or more times. Look—with honesty and objectivity—for any telltale signs that may show your nervousness. Sure, some will be seen—a fumbled word, a repeated gesture, a silly smile. But most of those little signs of stage fright will not be noticed by most viewers. You'll spot them, you'll worry about them, you'll feel your own nervousness—but your audience rarely does. After all, how often do you notice the signs of nervousness shown by your minister, teacher, TV newscaster when they speak? One reason you don't is:

3. With experience, stage fright is almost always reduced.

After you've given even just one speech, you'll realize that your greatest fear—fear of failure—just doesn't come true. You'll do better—virtually all speakers do better—on your first speech than you probably think you will.

"But what if my mind goes completely blank?" beginning speakers often ask. "Suppose I fumble a word and it comes out dirty? Or insulting? What if I make a fool of myself? What if . . ."

The fact is, such problems rarely—*very* rarely—happen. Have you ever witnessed such a case? Have you ever actually seen a speaker lose track entirely of what he's talking about? Have you ever heard a word fumbled so badly the speech, or the speaker, was destroyed?

Don't point to the goofs on TV shows. Many of those errors are written into the scripts. They're planted to give the program color, spontaneity, a gimmick. I've watched nearly a dozen different network TV shows in rehearsals as professionals carefully plotted the wording, timing, placement of those apparent "errors."

Still, the really worried speaker asks, "But what about that famous radio announcer who fumbled the name of the President of the United States?" That was some fifty years ago!—Harry Von Zell introducing President Herbert Hoover as "President Hoobert Hever."

What about all those horrible goofs on those Blooper Records?

Sure, embarrassing fumbles do happen. But rarely. Think of all the speakers you've heard—TV newscasters, politicians, religious leaders, teachers, salespersons, lecturers, and more. You'll be hard-pressed to come up with a single example of a serious, significant goof that you've heard yourself. The point: Errors happen, but they get retold and elaborated upon far beyond their actual frequency and importance.

Besides, you can turn an error or fumble to your advantage by using humor and keeping your cool. If you fumble a word, or several in a row, you might use one of the many old gags which still get a laugh, such as:

Let me try that again—this time, in English!

Sorry, my tongue gets tied up when I open my mouth and it sees so many good-looking people.

Guess I need a new set of teeth!

They told me not to buy teeth at a hardware store!

After you've given your first speech, you'll continue to learn that stage fright really isn't that big a problem. Sure, you'll still be nervous. But you'll continue to gain control of your nerves. The reason? You'll gradually begin to:

4. Realize that your audience is there to hear you succeed, not fail.

Think of your own reactions when you're a member of an audience. In the moments before the speaker begins, what goes through your mind? Do you think, *Sure hope this is a lousy speaker! Hope he does a poor job. Hope he's a failure!!*

Of course you don't think such negative thoughts.

You, virtually all listeners, think just the opposite. We hope that the speaker we are about to hear will be interesting, stimulating, informative, entertaining, persuasive. We hope that this time we'll hear a speech of value. We hope to hear something that will benefit us, that we can tell others about with pride, even making them envious that they've missed this speech.

This empathy between speaker and listeners, between actor and audience, is the surest relief from stage fright, according to psychoanalyst Donald M. Kaplan. Once you as the speaker receive that first positive reaction from an audience, you'll suddenly feel much more confident, relaxed. When you first see some of your listeners nod in agreement with something you say, much of your stage fright will disappear immediately. That's one major reason why so many experienced speakers often begin their talks by telling a joke—the laughter from the audience relaxes both the speaker and his listeners.

Another way to look at nervousness is that it's "nature's way" of helping a speaker be alert, sharp, up to doing a good job. It is like the pre-game jitters of the athlete. Once the football player makes his first contact, once the baseball player chases that first hit, almost all nervousness is gone. Now they are concentrating on success. The roar of the crowd tells them the fans are there to see success, to watch a winning team.

Listeners look forward to a successful speech in the same way. The athlete concentrates on the game, on winning, on success. Such focusing on a desirable end result will help the speaker, too. Therefore:

5. Concentrate on WHAT you're saying, not on HOW you're saying it.

The British TV talk host, David Frost, asked Broadway musical comedy star, Carol Channing, "On opening night, do you get nervous?" Her reply: "I don't call it nervousness—I prefer to call it concentration."

By concentrating on the ideas, the importance, the relevance of what you're telling your audience, you'll further control and reduce your nervousness. Think, *More than anything else at this moment, I want these listeners to get what I have to say to them.*

But instead, many speakers focus their thoughts on insignificant, detracting details. The beginner worries about using just exactly the right word. A voice that sounds quavery to the speaker becomes another point to worry about, even though the audience can't spot such minor voice changes. Gestures, movement, emphasis, sentence structure, all such relatively minor factors become mountains in the minds of many speakers.

Don't let such details distract you. Focus on the "big picture"—on your message, not your delivery.

6. Let your nervousness have an outlet.

There is no valid reason to try to hold back your nervousness, to attempt to block it or hold it strictly within yourself. Just let your nervousness be.

One effective outlet for many is talking about it. Paul Newman spoke openly about his nervousness about serving as master-of-ceremonies for President Carter's inaugural gala. "We all have butterflies, but with the new President there, it felt like the butterflies in our stomachs had the teeth of crocodiles!" Lee Meriwether, star of the TV show *Barnaby Jones* and former Miss America, says, "I still get very jittery before a show or a public appearance." Says Dinah Shore: "You've got to be a little nervous."

Such professionals, knowing they're going to be nervous, develop their own outlets. Some simply wring their hands. Others meditate. Deep breathing helps.

Many speakers find relaxation exercises helpful. Breathe deeply a dozen or so times every fifteen minutes during the hour or two before you give a speech.

Another technique: A few minutes prior to going before your audience, sit in a chair—preferably in a room where you're alone—and move your head from side to side as far as it will go. Stretching those muscles should help you relax. Do that maybe ten times. Then let your head go forward, down toward your chest, as far as you can, then back—way back, until you're looking almost straight up. Do that about ten times. Finally, rotate your head. Move it in circles from left to right, then from right to left, several times. Relaxation exercises such as these help many speakers—beginners as well as pros—keep their cool, hang loose, calm down at least a bit.

Sammy Davis, Jr. relaxes just before going on stage

by methodically selecting the rings he'll wear. One speaker visualizes his audience in a ridiculous situation so that his speech will be a welcome improvement— sometimes he thinks of them perched in trees, or dressed only in underwear, or standing on a fast-melting iceberg.

Some speakers smoke. Some nonsmokers hold a cigarette just to give their hands something to do. Many pace. I catnap.

Another outlet is "floating," recommended by Dr. Claire Weekes, a leading medical expert on nerves. In a *Reader's Digest* article she wrote: "If your body trembles, let it tremble. Don't feel obliged to try to stop it. Don't even strive for relaxation. Don't be too concerned because you are tense and cannot relax."

In essence, if you'll just quit being nervous about nervousness, you won't be as nervous!

Still, there's one more step to controlling stage fright which is far more effective than all others. This next —final—step will build your self-confidence on a truly solid base. It is—

7. Preparation!

Clearly, if you prepare carefully you'll greatly reduce your concern about what you're going to say. Your nervousness will be easier to control. Prepare effectively and you'll feel more like you're really ready to speak. Your ideas will be more firmly set in your mind. You'll have your facts stored in your memory bank. Preparation will help make you confident.

But there's one big problem many of us face as we prepare a speech. We think, *Gee, if I only had a few extra days to prepare I could give a REALLY good speech!* If you had a few more facts about the cost of that new dam, for example, your speech would be truly impressive. You could get those facts by phoning your senator's office but then the information would probably have to be looked up, then sent to you by mail. You just don't have the time.

If you have a few days to prepare a speech, you soon feel that a week would be better. If you have a month to prepare, two months would give you time to really present a good speech.

But you simply must face your time schedule. Prepare as best you can in the time you have. Wishing won't bring you more time. But **preparing efficiently** will help you use what time you have as best you can. Use the list of checkpoints below, to review the steps you can take in controlling stage fright, before you speak.

Here's the next step. But first:

The next page presents a check-off guide of how to control your stage fright. There'll be a list of checkpoints at the end of each step in preparing a speech. Use them to help you be sure you're as prepared as you need to be for each of your speeches.

CHECKPOINTS:
CONTROL YOUR STAGE FRIGHT

Check off each point listed below as you prepare your speeches.

_____ 1. Recognize that you are not alone in suffering from stage fright.

_____ 2. Realize we all appear much more confident than we feel.

_____ 3. Understand that with experience, your stage fright will be reduced.

_____ 4. Accept the fact that your audience will be there to hear you succeed, not fail.

_____ 5. Concentrate on WHAT you're to say, not on how you're to say it.

_____ 6. Use an outlet for your nerves—wringing your hands, pacing, meditating, chewing gum.

_____ 7. Prepare your speeches as completely as is realistic under the time you've got, the facts you have, etc.

4

STEP #2: Select
Your Subject

> The secret of being a bore is
> to tell everything.
>
> VOLTAIRE

YOU HAVE JUST returned from a visit to some other
company or organization. Very likely you'll then meet
informally with your boss or president or whoever to
relate a bit of what you observed. That meeting might
well conclude with your receiving an invitation—or an
order—to give a speech. Perhaps you'll be told something like this:

So that's how they do that over there! Listen, at next
week's meeting of our group, how about giving us a
talk about it—OK?

At first, that may sound like a pretty clear, specific
direction for your talk. But later, as you sit down to
think through just what you are going to say, you'll find
there are some tough questions to answer.

* Should your talk simply tell the group "how they
  do that over there"—what you saw during your
  visit?
* Should you report the problems you heard about
  after the visit?

21

* Should you urge others to make the visit?
* Are you expected to convince your associates that they, too, should be doing whatever it is you observed?
* Or just maybe you should talk about the . . .

As you can see, that invitation to speak gave you a lot of space to decide for yourself just what the emphasis of your speech should be.

You wouldn't have to make those decisions if you'd been invited to give the talk with specific instructions such as:

Good visit, huh? Fine! Better get our group together and give them a talk on why they should start planning now for that new procedure.

With that invitation—or order—to speak, you know exactly what your speech is supposed to do for your audience—get them to "start planning now for that new procedure."

This is an important point in planning an effective speech. Unless you decide what effect your words are to have on your listeners, your talk will usually lack direction and, consequently, effectiveness. Consider some other examples.

You're supervising a youth group and your sponsor tells you:

Look, those guys have been getting away with that for far too long! Now things are really out of hand. You get them together and give them a talk—now!

Should your speech review rules already established? Or present new rules? Should you warn the group that some may have to be dropped if things get "out of hand" again? Do you give instructions or make an appeal? Should you base your talk on group spirit, individual responsibility, cost to the organization, or what?

Another situation: You may have taken an unusual

trip recently, told the program chairman of a club about it, and then been asked: "Do come and tell our club about it next week, will you?"

Should your talk get members to sign up to take such a trip? Should you warn them of the problems? Show pictures? Make the trip sound attractive, or not?

You need to answer such questions—*you need to determine what effect your speech is to have on your audience*—in order to select the content of your speech. That, in turn, means you need to word the subject of your talk in very exact, specific terms. To do that, follow this two-step process:

TO PICK THE SUBJECT FOR YOUR TALK:

1. Make an analysis of the speaking situation—the audience, the occasion, yourself as the speaker—then:
2. Decide exactly what you want your talk to *DO* to that audience.

Analyzing Your Audience

Bloomingdale's, the famous New York department store, is a "phenomenal success," according to a *Time* cover story, because of its "essential formula": "First, know your customer, his age, affluence, customs, habits, tastes."

Such an analysis is even more important for the public speaker. Rather than the one-to-one sales talk by a clerk to a customer in a department store, the public speaker is trying to influence an audience composed of many diverse listeners.

One speaker with some experience told me, "Sure, I analyze my audience. After I'm introduced, I stand up there at the lectern and I take my time for as long as I feel I can—looking them over, sizing them up."

Fine. But that's too late. And too shallow.

The speaker's analysis of an audience should be made long before stepping up to speak. You should study your audience before you decide anything more than your general topic. A careful, detailed analysis of your listeners should be the basis of your decisions of exactly what points you will present, which kinds of evidence —statistics, stories, comparisons, and such—you will use. Even your style of delivery should be influenced by your audience.

There are ten questions to be answered for such an analysis.

1. What does that audience already know about the subject of your talk?

A problem being talked about a lot in California is whether high schools should set aside a specific room in which students can smoke. Now assume you were moved to present your views about that topic before two audiences—the Board of Trustees of your local high school and your community's medical association. While your viewpoint would remain the same for both talks, the content should certainly be quite different. For the school board you should probably present at least some statistics and case studies about the health hazards of smoking. For your audience of doctors, however, such facts should not be presented because they already know them. Your talk to the doctors might be an appeal for them to help support your views.

Usually the best way to find out what your audience already knows about the topic of your talk is to ask the person who invites you to speak. Ask if the group has already had other speakers on the same subject. Does the group have a committee or a study group concerned with the topic? Are there experts in that audience who may know even more than you do?

2. What is your audience's attitude toward your subject?

Not long ago a friend of mine spoke to a service club which helps students with visual handicaps. His subject:

the need for special schools for youngsters born blind. His problem: He didn't know that the club supports integrating such students in regular classes rather than separating them. If he had known this—and he certainly should have before planning his speech—he could have given a speech capitalizing on that audience's viewpoint. He could have emphasized the special problems blind children have when playing with sighted youngsters; he might have pointed to ways the students might learn faster if studying and associating with others with similar problems. Instead, without knowing his audience's attitude, he plunged in with a case directly opposing the listeners' view. The polite—but light—applause as he finished his speech was his first tip-off that his speech was not successful.

Before planning a speech, you can find out your audience's attitude toward your topic by asking the person who invited you to speak. Or ask a member. Or, perhaps, ask the president of the group. If you're talking to a government agency—city council, school board, or county commission—you could look up the public records to find how each member voted on this or related problems.

Sure, that's a lot of work. Many speeches aren't worth that trouble. But some are.

President Reagan's success in winning support for many of his programs can be attributed, in many cases, to careful analysis of his listeners' attitudes toward a subject prior to making a speech. He asked his staff to keep day-to-day tabulations of just how every senator and every representative was planning to vote on the sale of AWACS planes to Saudi Arabia. Based on those reports of the attitudes of potential voters, the President planned how he'd talk to various groups of legislators. Those reports also helped other government officials—including then Secretary of State Alexander Haig and Secretary of Defense Caspar Weinberger—plan their speeches, too.

3. What is your audience's attitude toward YOU as the speaker?

If you're 5'5" and weigh 200 pounds, you'll have a bit of difficulty giving a talk on the need for physical fitness. On the other hand, if you weighed 300 pounds a year ago, that audience might very well accept you as an authority.

Try another tack. Does your audience, or at least some of them, already know your views? Perhaps they read about your ideas in the local paper, reported when you've spoken before to other groups. If you work for an oil company and intend to speak to a taxpayers' group about reducing the costs of government, you'd better recognize that many in the audience will also be concerned about the high costs apparently imposed by your company.

You'll be able to design a more effective speech if you know ahead of time if your listeners are likely to be receptive to your ideas because of your own reputation, their impression of the job you hold, or other groups to which you belong.

4. What are the occupations of your listeners?

If your audience is composed of mostly structural engineers, or housewives, or school administrators, or travel agents, or any other group with common experiences, education, interests, or background, then your talk can build on that unifying background.

But most audiences are composed of people with a wide variety of occupations. This makes it more difficult for you to select the specifics of your speech. While engineers may be impressed by your statistics, educators may be convinced more easily and surely by human interest stories.

5. What's the economic status of your audience?

An audience made up of people with comfortable incomes may be interested in tax-shelter plans to help them reduce their taxes. But if you talk about those same tax-shelter plans to people who are less than wealthy, many will reject your subject as being a "tax loophole."

If you plan to speak about the need to fight the government's cutbacks in food stamps, you should know the precise economic status of your audience. If your listeners have high incomes and pay high taxes, they'll likely want those food stamps reduced. If your audience is made up of many people with below-average incomes, they may want food stamps increased.

If your subject is how to select a fishing pole, the status of research on solar energy, the impact of automatic typewriters, or some other neutral topic, then the economic status of your audience might not influence your speech.

6. What is the educational level of your listeners?

Consider these facts:

* The average adult in America has but slightly more than a high school education.
* Four out of every ten adults have not graduated from high school.
* Nearly three million Americans can't read or write any language.
* One out of eight of our citizens has less than four years of education.
* About twenty percent of the youngsters in the fifth grade today will not graduate from high school.

How do you use such knowledge about your audiences to design your speeches? Consider these examples:

* A sales talk about life insurance to assembly line workers should explain the need for insurance in much more basic, graphic terms than when the audience is a group of librarians. Neither group may know much about insurance, but the higher education of librarians will help them understand complex points faster.
* A speech telling a committee of college students why they should join a movement to stop the building of any more apartment houses in a crowded area should make the points more broadly than a speech on the same subject to a meeting of local architects—for them, you can get pretty technical about such details as stress–strain factors, land-use ratios, and interior–exterior interacts.

In such speaking situations, you adapt your speech to the appropriate educational level of your listeners. The appropriate level for a speech is usually at or just a bit higher than that of your listeners. If you speak over their heads—use a lot of quotes from 18th-century literature when talking to a group of TV repairmen—they'll often be turned off by your speech. And if you speak below the level of your audience—explaining to a group of experienced cross-country skiers how to select their first pair of learning skis—again you'll probably have an audience that pays little attention to what you say.

The point is: If you know your audience, you should be able to give a speech to them that will be more effective. But remember—knowing your audience should not lead you to change the point of your speech. Rather, knowing your audience should guide you as you select the data to support your view, pick the words you use, and determine the complexity of the ideas you present.

7. What's the cultural status of your audience?

Are most in your audience likely to be regular readers of magazines such as the *New Yorker, Atlantic,*

Harper's? Or might they usually read *Modern Screen,* or *True Romances?*

On a Saturday afternoon, do your listeners take their kids to watch a local ball game played by a team sponsored by the nearby auto dealer? Or do they tour a museum? Do they watch TV at night, or might they go out to the local art theater to see a foreign film?

You may be asked to give a speech, for example, about your trip to Europe. If the cultural status of your audience is such that eating out at a fast-food diner is a big event, then your stories about the fine restaurants of Paris might not catch their interest.

Figuring out the cultural status of your listeners can even help you pick the clothes you wear when you give a speech. Next week I'll put on a necktie for the second time in more than six months—I'm speaking to a state convention of leaders of chambers of commerce. They're a rather sophisticated audience. If I dress up a bit, they might listen to my ideas a bit more carefully. The week after, I'm talking to a group of writers. For them I'll wear my usual casual, comfortable, open-necked sports shirt.

The point, once again: *Know your audience.* Then adjust your speaking to them and chances can be significantly higher that your speech will have the impact you want to make on your listeners.

8. What's the sex of your audience?

Despite liberation movements, most audiences, most individuals, still recognize and accept differences between audiences of men, women, or mixed audiences. Most speakers would want to talk a bit differently to a group of girl-scout leaders than to a team of construction workers.

Suppose you're to give talks to both those audiences —the girl-scout leaders and then a team of construction workers. Your subject: the need for their help in rebuilding a trailer park for the elderly, which was recently ruined by floods. To the girl-scout leaders, your speech might well include the point that their womanly understanding of helping people is needed for this project. To the construction workers, one of the main points of your speech might be that they are the best source in town for the manly skills and strength needed to do the heavy construction work.

"That's sexist!" you claim? You may be right. Still, most people react most favorably to speeches which recognize their own distinctive qualities.

Pardon the repetition, but the basic point is so important: K-n-o-w y-o-u-r a-u-d-i-e-n-c-e. Coaches often make the same point as they tell their teams, "Know the game, sure—but more important, know your player!"

9. What's the age of your audience?

Just out of college? About to retire? Already retired? Or, more likely, a cross section of various age groups?

If your talk is about "the" war, recognize that for thirty-year-olds that means the Vietnam War. To the forty-five-year-olds, "the" War was the Korean War. But for sixty-year-olds, it was World War II.

10. How many will be in your audience?

A small, intimate group of, say, twenty or less? Then you can gather them in a circle and talk with them informally. Or a couple hundred or more listeners? Then you'll have to project your voice or use a public address system.

If your topic is to be counseling techniques, your sitting informally as part of a small group of listeners will enhance your ability to talk about those techniques. With a large audience you might have to present much more dramatic examples because you'll not have as much personal contact with your listeners. Charts, drawings, or other visuals can be sketched casually on a chalkboard for a small audience. A large group would need visuals of considerable size if they were to be seen at all.

Your job, then, is to **get as much information about your audience as you can,** to help guide you in the selection of the content and presentation of your speech. You'd not change your views, but should change how you present and illustrate those views.

Analyzing the Occasion

A few years ago I gave a speech to the members of a Southern California service club to convince them that they should support the building of an educational television station in the community. Just before I spoke, the group voted on that very issue. Fortunately, they agreed to support the station. I quickly adapted my speech. I shortened it. And I changed my points from reasons why they should endorse the project, to reasons why they'd just made a wise decision.

Obviously, I'd goofed. Before planning my speech I had not completed a sufficiently detailed analysis of the occasion at which I was to speak. Some people may argue that the program chairman who invited me to speak should have warned me that a vote would be taken before I spoke. But I'm responsible for the success of my own speech. I should do all I can to insure it is effective.

One important step to help a speaker be sure his speech is appropriate for the occasion at which he is to speak is to analyze the speaking situation. There are six points to consider:

1. What is the purpose of the meeting?

Has the audience gathered just to hear your talk? Or, are they there to hear speeches by others, too? Might there be speakers with opposing views? Is it a community conference? A regular business meeting? A cultural affair? Perhaps a celebration of an historic event?

Are the listeners there to be entertained? Are they expecting a humorous speech about an interesting trip you've made? Or are you to kid one of the members in a popular roasting which some groups consider to be an honor for someone?

Or is the purpose of the meeting informative? Are you to provide the audience with new insights? New information? Are you to present a new proposal or problem?

Maybe your audience is there to be persuaded. Should you present a solid factual case? Or a hard sell? Or should you guide them to a decision by gentle implications?

In sum, just what is it you expect **your audience** to get out of this meeting?

2. Where will the meeting be held?

One college I know of tries to encourage students to attend meetings by having guest speakers talk in an open room, just to the side of the cafeteria, during the noon hour. The idea is that students passing by on their way to lunch may tarry long enough to get interested in the speech, enter the room, and become a part of the audience. But the speakers must compete with a constant flow of students. The students are usually more interested in eating than listening. Speakers have to talk over the constant clatter of dishes banging in the adjacent kitchen. It's a mighty difficult location for a speaker to try to present ideas. An analysis of the speaking situation should tell most speakers they'd better turn down the invitation to talk there.

Another difficult speaking location is the chambers of the city council at a nearby community. A new city hall was built just last year. The meeting room is truly spectacular—modern, luxurious, colorful. It has an elaborate lectern location on a level lower than that of the desks of the council. The result: A speaker appearing before the group feels greatly inhibited. His back is to most people in the audience. He faces the five councilmen as though they were a superior tribunal.

So a speaker should find out about the physical setting in which he is to speak. Then he may adapt his speaking style. He or she can get mentally ready for the situation.

3. What facilities will there be for you?

Will there be a lectern? Public address system? Chalkboard? Will the chairs be set in rows, or can they be moved into a circle, for example, so you can create a more informal speaking situation?

Will the room be air-conditioned? If your talk is to be given late in the summer, will that air conditioner make the room too cool for your audience, thereby distracting their minds from your words? Will that air conditioner be noisy, making it harder to hear you?

What other equipment, furniture, might be there to help or to hinder your talk? A tape recorder is popular as a regular installation in many speaking situations today. But some people in your audience, and perhaps you yourself, may be inhibited by having your exact wording reproduced.

4. When will you give your talk?

At the end of a long, boring business meeting? Just before a recess for refreshments? After a heated debate over the location of next week's party?

Consider the typical meeting of teachers. Almost always, it is held at the end of their workday. They've been struggling with students all day. They've been trying to be alert, creative, productive for six or so hours. Then, along about four in the afternoon, the teachers are called together to hear a speaker. Most of the faculty are thoroughly tired from the day's labors. Many are

starting to think about dinner. They're worrying about
when they're going to grade papers and about other
subjects unrelated to the speech they now have to hear.

Furthermore, how long is your talk to be? Will you
have time to present just a brief rundown of your ideas?
Or will you have enough time to present a case supported with data?

5. What other events are on the program?

Will that audience be voting on who to send to a
conference in Hawaii? How much to raise the dues?
Other decisions that might detract from the impact of
your talk?

Will there be entertainment? A belly dancer, scheduled right after your talk, can do more to make minds
drift away from your words than all efforts you make
to be interesting, informative, and persuasive. In such
a case, you'd better make your speech informal, even
humorous if you can. Or if the entertainment clearly de-
tracts from what you want to say, ask if you can speak
at some other time. Or, try to get the entertainment
moved to another time.

Perhaps the biggest surprise a speaker can face is
showing up to give a speech and finding out just before
the meeting is to start that another speaker will be
present to give the opposite viewpoint. If you're getting
into a debate, you better find out about it before you
plan your speech.

6. What's after your speech?

Will there be questions from the audience? A free
dinner all those listeners want to get to as soon as you
stop speaking?

Will the audience take a vote after your speech, to
accept or reject your proposal? Might they decide to
set up a study committee to follow up on what you tell
them? Might they? . . .

You get the idea: There are a lot of factors which can influence the effectiveness of your talk. Knowing as much as you can about them before you plan your speech can help you give a better speech. You'll be able to prepare yourself better. Furthermore, you might be able to influence some other features on the program. Maybe, for example, you can get the group to hold off voting on the issue of your speech until after you've spoken.

Analyzing Yourself as the Speaker

I'm the first to admit that I'm not an accomplished public speaker. My own speech-making ability from a text is not first class. Some of the texts have not been good. I've used that format, and the consequences are I have developed a bad reputation both as to speeches and presentation.

That revealing self-analysis was made by a veteran of twenty-eight years of public speaking, a successful candidate in fourteen elections, the then President of the United States, Gerald Ford. He made it in the summer of 1976, shortly before he was to start a losing campaign.

Your analysis of yourself as a speaker need not be that self-deprecating nor that public. To help you plan your speech, your analysis should emphasize the practicalities you must face in preparing your speech. Your answers to the following four questions will help.

1. Do you have enough knowledge about the subject of your talk?

"You've just come back from a trip to England? Say, why don't you give a talk to our sewing club—we're studying British quilting."

Many travelers receive that kind of invitation. The inviter should know that simply visiting a country and having a skill in sewing, for example, does not prepare one for speaking about sewing in that country.

Businessmen are asked to speak on how to control inflation. Even though they may have important positions in major corporations, their jobs alone do not necessarily qualify them to speak on economics. Such businessmen should not accept those invitations to speak.

Consider another frequently faced situation. A speaker will read an article which effectively states his or her viewpoint on a subject. The article then becomes the structure and content for his or her speech. Why didn't such a speaker simply make copies of the article and distribute them to the audience? Certainly, at the very least, a speaker should add something of his or her own insights, facts, or organization of the material.

Ask yourself if you really know enough about the subject to give a talk which will be of value to your listeners. Indeed, you may have to do some additional research. You may have to do some further thinking. But certainly most of the content and structure of a speech should be your own. If not, you should simply refer your audience to a good source and not waste their time.

2. Do you have enough time to prepare your talk?

Even the President of the United States, with his staff of professional speech-writers who are in turn backed up by a crew of researchers, even he has a deadline to meet for his speeches. He, too, must plan well ahead to be sure he and the staff have time to prepare his speeches.

One good way to answer this question is to make a time-line. That's an engineer's projection of what tasks you have to do and how much time you'll need for each. Write, down, in sequence, such points as:

TASK	TIME
Analyzing the speaking situation	¼ hour
Selecting your speech purpose	¼ hour
Gathering your ideas and information	2 hours
Designing the beginning of your speech	¼ hour
Organizing your material	?
Designing the ending of your speech	?
Practicing your speech	?
Arranging for visuals, etc.	?
Other details?	?

Then find the time in your regular schedule to do each of these steps. Perhaps you can break away from your routine and take half a day and get most of the speech preparation completed. Or maybe you're so busy with your job and your other commitments that you'll have to stretch your speech preparation over several days. You might grab half an hour here, an hour there. In any event, try to schedule your preparation so you'll not be traveling to the audience while still thinking up things to say, still practicing how to say them.

3. Are you really interested in the speech subject?

Almost every rule on how to give a good speech has a few exceptions—except this one: *You MUST be sincerely interested in your subject if you are to give a good speech.*

A disc jockey broadcasting on a central California radio station, a friend of mine, is living proof of this rule. He's well into middle-age. For years he wandered, as do many radio announcers, from station to station, looking for that big break. When I first knew him, he was a so-so announcer on a tiny station in a small desert town. He was going nowhere. Finally he backed off, took a hard look and listened to himself. He came to realize he was actually trying to fake it. He didn't really believe in the products he was announcing—selling. He took leave from his job. He studied himself and other announcers. He talked with other professionals. With a new approach, he moved to still another station. Now he announced commercials only after he used the products. He now studied each one. He visited the plants where the products were made. He toured the stores where they were sold. Result: Though he's not really big-time—he caught his lack of sincerity a bit late in his announcing career—he is much more successful than he had been. Now he has a large, steady audience. He gets an above-average salary. Most important, he says, "Now I feel good about what I tell my listeners!"

It is true that some very polished professionals can fake an interest in a subject, some speakers can sound as if they are concerned about a topic when they really have little or no interest in it. Yet most professionals emphasize the need to be sincerely interested in what they talk about. Announcers, salespersons, politicians, teachers, lawyers, all types who are paid to talk, support this rule.

4. What's your reputation as a speaker, as an authority on the subject of your talk?

Will you be accepted by your listeners as knowledgeable, reliable and authoritative on the topic you're about to select for your speech?

Many beginning speakers respond, "Heck, I'm not an authority on anything!" But certainly you are an authority on your own feelings, ideas, impressions. A quick study about atomic power plants may not make you an expert, but no one knows better than you your own attitude about them.

Speak on subjects related to your own occupation, profession, hobbies, interests, and personal experience. Then you will be accepted by your audience as authoritative.

This Step #2 in preparing to speak urges you to select the subject for your speech by:

1. Analyzing your audience.
2. Analyzing the speaking situation.
3. Analyzing yourself as a speaker.

Now you need to decide exactly what you want your speech to *DO* to your audience.

CHECKPOINTS:
SELECT YOUR SUBJECT

As you prepare your speeches, check off each point listed below.

_____ Analysis of audience completed?
   _____ 1. Considered what they already know?
   _____ 2. Considered audience's attitude toward your speech subject?
   _____ 3. Figured out their attitude toward you as the speaker?
   _____ 4. Identified their occupations?
   _____ 5. Got an idea of their economic status?
   _____ 6. Found out their general educational level?
   _____ 7. Estimated their cultural status?
   _____ 8. Will there be all men? All women? Mixed audience?
   _____ 9. General age of most of your listeners?
   _____ 10. Number of people you'll be speaking to?
_____ Analysis of the occasion completed?
   _____ 1. What's the purpose of the meeting?
   _____ 2. Where will the meeting be held?
   _____ 3. Found out what facilities will be there for you?
   _____ 4. When will you give your talk?
   _____ 5. Found out what else is on the program?
   _____ 6. What's after your speech?
_____ Analysis of yourself as the speaker completed?
   _____ 1. Do you have enough knowledge about the subject of your talk?
   _____ 2. Do you have enough time to prepare?

_____ 3. Are you really interested in the speech subject?

_____ 4. Will the audience accept you as a knowledgeable speaker?

5

STEP #3: Gather Your Ideas and Information

It is easy for men to talk one thing and think another.

PUBLILIUS SYRUS

TO GET IDEAS and information for your speech, the first thing you should do is rush right down to your local library—right?

Wrong!

The first source for the content of your speech should be *your own head*. Start by thinking through what you already know about your speech subject.

Jot down all the facts and points that come to mind. Make just rough notes. Write your ideas in whatever order you think of them. Don't worry about the sequence. Sorting them out into some logical pattern will be easy if you wait until later. You'll learn how in the next steps.

As you think through what you've got in mind on the subject of your speech, you may find you really don't have much to say. Perhaps all you have is a concern about a problem. Maybe you have just a few facts that you read in a newspaper article, for example. And that's all you have for content for your speech. What do you do then?

Then you may be in trouble.

A speech should present *your* ideas, *your* views. Or

it should present facts and figures *you've* discovered. At the very least, your speech should present your own new structure or understanding of a subject or problem.

Let's work with an example. Say you've been concerned about your local taxes. They keep going up. Now your city council has just announced a budget for next year which you consider just too much. You feel you must speak out against their spending of your money.

Start by writing down your ideas and the information you already have to back up your ideas. Your first rough list might look like this:

---

1. Citizens can't keep paying more!
2. My taxes went up too much last year—get copies of my tax bills for last two years.
3. City plans which make no sense:
   (1) A million $ "transportation center" when we have no trains, few buses, a few beat-up taxis.
   (2) $91,000 for "improving walkways" because "people are driving less and walking more" (!!)
   (3) $3.6 million to widen a few blocks of a main street—the slight traffic bottleneck will just move down the road a bit farther!
4. Get copy of full budget—find more such items!
5. How come they keep talking about a long-range plan, but don't follow it?
6. $3.5 million for a bike path! It was first proposed about ten years ago—now interest in bike riding is falling—(get some figures).
7. Talk to each councilman—don't any see the stupidity of all this spending???
8. Check with Taxpayer's Association—what's their position this year?
9. _____.
10. _____.

As you can see, these points fall into three types:

1. Facts and figures you already have.
2. Sources for more—the councilmen, etc.
3. Facts you'll have to get from other sources—example: Point #2. You should find out how your tax increase compares with others in nearby towns which are comparable with yours.

In that example, it looks like you have your particular information—concerns, ideas—pretty well in mind. But you'll need a lot more information—data, facts, specifics.

Specifics in a speech serve four purposes. If you'll think for a moment, you'll probably be able to name those purposes yourself. They are:

1. Specifics *prove* a point.
2. Specifics *clarify* a point.
3. Specifics make a point *memorable*.
4. Specifics *add interest* to your speech.

In planning your speech, it will help to keep those purposes in mind.

Here's how specifics work for you in a speech.

Consider that first purpose of specifics—to *prove a point*. Suppose you claim in your speech, "My taxes keep going up year after year!" You can prove that point simply by presenting the figures you have on your tax bills from the last few years.

The second purpose of specifics in a speech is to help you *clarify a point*. One of your points might be, "Building a transportation center is ridiculous!" To clarify what you mean by that, you might present a bus schedule showing just how few buses come and go each day. You might then point to other towns like yours which have more buses and no city-built transportation center. You might check with bus companies and find out that they usually build their own bus stations, rather than getting tax-paid buildings. How you get such specifics we'll detail in a moment.

Specifics in a speech can make a point *memorable*. If you take the total cost of the tax package you're objecting to, divide it by the number of citizens in your town, you may come up with an impressive cost-per-citizen figure.

One year I gave a lot of speeches in support of building an educational television station in a city I used to live in. The total cost, a half-million dollars, is a mighty big figure, especially to educators who are used to worrying about budget items of a few hundred dollars. But that $500,000 became memorable when I did a few calculations and was able to tell them—accurately:

> The cost of our half-million dollar TV station works out to less than what most of our students spend in a year on just paper and pencils!

That specific comparison was the one fact most remembered in my speeches. It was quoted repeatedly in articles reporting my speeches. That data was memorable. (And that station was built!)

Finally, specifics *add interest to your speech.* Widening a street might well be of little interest to citizens who don't drive on it often. But you might really get them interested if you use a map to show that traffic will soon be moving into other parts of town as drivers search for shortcuts around the new location of the bottleneck—shortcuts that may increase traffic past the homes of people who don't think this is their problem.

So that's what specifics can do for your speech. Now consider the various *types of specifics* you can present:

1. Examples
2. Quotations
3. Statistics
4. Stories
5. Definitions
6. Comparisons
7. Contrasts
8. Audiovisual aids

A warning: Not all of those types of information can be used equally as well for each of the four purposes of data you've just read. You have to select your information depending on your needs and the speaking situation. A good illustration of that problem comes with that first type of information.

1. Examples

These are one of the most frequently used—and misused—types of information. Pope John Paul II used an effective example in a speech he gave when he visited Hiroshima, Japan: "For example, it has been estimated that about half of the world's research workers are at present employed for military purposes."

But consider this use of an example from a speech given by a student in one of my classes: "Our state camp grounds are too crowded. Last weekend we went camping in a state park, and the tents and trailers were so close together we had no privacy."

That example explains what the speaker means by "too crowded." The example also makes the point a bit more memorable—listeners can visualize the problems of people camping close to one another. And that example also serves the fourth purpose of specifics—to add interest to a speech—people like to hear about what others do on vacations.

But remember, there's another purpose in using specifics in a speech—to prove a point.

An example is NOT valid proof!

That's how so very many speakers misuse an example. They'll say such things as: "I know that dealer is dishonest. Just last week he gave my sister the wrong change for a ten-dollar bill."

That's an ineffective—incorrect—use of an example because the speaker is trying to convince listeners on the basis of just one isolated experience.

To use an example to prove a point, the speaker needs to show that the example is truly representative of conditions as they are most of the time. Do customers *often* get the wrong change from that dealer? If so, the speaker's proven his point—the dealer is dishonest. If shortchanging happens only occasionally, the dealer may still be dishonest, but a few examples don't prove him so.

So *do* use examples in your speeches. They're valuable. Interesting. But if you use examples to try to prove a point, be sure the examples show a true picture of the situation.

2. Quotations

A speaker is using a quotation when he presents a statement made by someone else. Usually it's from a person who is an authority or who has special experience with the subject.

Quotations can range from ones you may pick up yourself—"Just yesterday one of the foremen told me, 'These machines are wearing out.'"

Or, quotations can be dug out of research reports, reference materials, books, and such. But that's not as hard to do as you may think.

Your library—even the smallest library—usually has at least several reference books which list quotations by subject. The best reference is *Familiar Quotations* by John Bartlett. First published in 1855, it is now in its fifteenth edition, runs to 1,540+ pages. Nearly a third of the book consists of an index to help you find a suitable quotation on just about every subject. If you're preparing a speech about taxes, for example, you'll find quotations by such people as Shakespeare, Sir Walter Scott, and Franklin Delano Roosevelt.

Another way to get quotations for your speeches is to collect your own—not only when you're preparing to give a speech, but gathered as you come across them. If you give speeches now and then, it may be worth your time to jot down good quotations whenever you find ones that relate to your job, hobbies, or whatever subjects you might speak on.

For example, when getting ready to write this book,

I knew I'd need some quotations from current speakers. One day I was skimming through the magazine *Vital Speeches*. It publishes the full scripts of notable speeches. The following quotation interested me. I jotted it down, in case I could use it some time. I've included it here to show how President Reagan used a quotation in one of his speeches. He gave the speech to the graduates of the class of 1981 at the U.S. Military Academy at West Point.

> In the sunset of his life, a West Point graduate, Douglas MacArthur, returned to this place to address the cadet corps. No one who ever heard him that day can ever forget his call to duty, honor, country. Nor his declaration that so long as there was breath in his body he would hear the words, "The Corps, the Corps, the Corps."

Quotations are valuable because they add authority to your speech. They tend to show that you're not alone in thinking as you do—that there are experts who say the same thing.

On the other hand, you probably know the big weakness in using quotes. Someone can almost always find someone else to quote who has said just the opposite. When Mediterranean fruit flies infested California orchards, politicians were busy quoting ecologists on the dangers of using sprays to get rid of the dangerous bugs. But other politicians quoted other ecologists who claimed the sprays were not harmful to humans. Who was a listener to believe?

The value of a quotation depends largely on who said it. If the person is knowledgeable, objective, and honest, the quotation may be accepted.

But it has become fashionable for some people to reject a quotation even when it is from someone who is a recognized authority. The words of a nuclear scientist, for example, stating that nuclear power plants are safe, are often rejected by some listeners because they feel the scientist has a vested interest in the power plant. And that may well be true. But many of those same listeners then accept quotations from, say, a college student in his first year of studying physics, as he claims nuclear power is unsafe.

As a speaker, your problem in using quotations is to try to determine whom you can quote that your listeners will believe. To decide that, go back again to your analysis of your audience. Whom might you quote who is admired by those listeners?

3. Statistics

Many listeners are interested and impressed by facts and figures. The head of the Federal Election Commission, John D. Aikens, started a long string of statistics in a speech by saying:

In the 1980 election, there were 2,266 candidates running for the Senate and House. They raised a combined total of $240.1 million.

But statistics, too, can cause problems for a speaker.

First, some listeners reject all statistics. "Figures can lie and liars can figure" is a popular line in some circles. But while that quote is a clever turn of words, it is so broad a generalization that it has little value in helping either a speaker or a listener decide whether or not to accept a particular statistic. So you have to move on to other criteria.

One basis on which to decide if you should use a particular statistic is to consider the source. Will your listeners believe whoever provided the figure? Go back to Step #2, in which you made an analysis of your audience. If your listeners are members of the same profession as the source of your statistic, your audience may believe your statistic. On the other hand, if you're speaking to a group of union members, they might not accept a statistic you use from a management source.

Another problem with statistics: They can be very dull! But they don't have to be. You as the speaker can word a statistic so it becomes interesting, even memorable. Consider this statistic:

* Nearly 37 million Americans move to a new home each year.

A fact, but not very interesting to most listeners. But you could present the same figure by saying:

* Each year the equivalent of our two most populous states—California and New York—move into new homes.

That wording should make many more of your listeners remember what you say.

President Reagan made a statistic memorable when he spoke to the Joint Session of Congress about his first budget. He said:

A few weeks ago I called such a figure—a trillion dollars—incomprehensible. I've been trying to think of a way to illustrate how big it really is. The best I could come up with is to say that a stack of $1,000 bills in your hand only four inches high would make you a millionaire. A trillion dollars would be a stack of $1,000 bills seventy-six miles high.

Few people remember the exact figures they hear in a speech. You can tell an audience the fact that in the late 1970s the United States was building some 75,000 new streets and roads a year. You'll make that figure more impressive if you point out that those roads would circle the world three times. In three years, that's more than the distance to the moon! Many of your listeners won't remember that figure, but chances are they'll remember something such as "Wow!—we're sure building a heck of a lot of roads!!"

Another technique to help your listeners remember numbers is to round them off. An audience doesn't need the exact figure. Instead of telling them that the latest population figure for Chicago is 3,049,479, tell them that a little more than three million people now live there. Sure, you dropped 49,479 people—about the population of Athens, Georgia, or Ames, Iowa. But you lowered the figure by less than two percent, statistically a small amount. And you made your basic figure much more memorable.

4. Stories

One of the main values in telling a story is that people like to hear about what happens to other people. And many listeners will be more impressed with stories than statistics.

For example, consider what many people think when a speaker says something such as:

If you think our local school administration is confused, let me tell you what happened when I telephoned the county schools office last week. First, I talked with a consultant, a Dr. . . .

Many in the audience will think, *Say, this sounds interesting! A story about something that happened to the speaker. Wonder how it turned out? I better keep listening.*

Other listeners will think, *Hey, this MUST be true—the speaker says it happened to her, and she's using a person's name!*

The major danger in telling stories is that many speakers stretch them out with far too many details. Don't you be a speaker who tells a story something like this:

So then I got in this guy's boat. And, like I said, it was a cold day. And there was some fog around—over the hills, but not out on the bay. Well, not out on the bay yet. And we'd brought a lunch to eat while we sailed. Boy, it was a good lunch—I'd bought a couple of special sandwiches at the Little Gourmet

Shop on the wharf, near where we kept the boat. While I was waiting for those sandwiches to be made, a fellow says to me, he says, . . .

Come on! listeners yell mentally at such a speaker. *Get to the point!*

5. Definitions

They are simply statements of what you mean when you use certain words or phrases.

Economist Milton Friedman, Professor at the University of Chicago, used a definition in a speech when he told an audience at Pepperdine University in California: "My subject is 'The Future of Capitalism.' When I speak of the future of capitalism I mean the future of competitive capitalism—a free enterprise capitalism."

The main value of a definition in a speech is to make sure you and your listeners are considering the same point.

In speeches presenting one side or the other of controversial issues, definitions are especially important. Try listening to a couple of people sitting around a table in a coffee shop, for example, as they talk about their ideas on some debatable topic. Don't let yourself get involved in the argument. Just listen. Carefully. Often, in just a few minutes, you'll hear that they only *seem* to have different opinions. What they're not agreeing on, really, may be definitions. One person might say, "How you voting on that gun issue—think we should have gun control?" Someone else may reply, "Sure—guns should be registered." Another joins in—"What? Take my guns away from me? Never!" And so they're into an argument they'll never end until they agree on just what they mean by "gun control."

In using definitions in speeches, *don't* follow the words of British writer Lewis Carroll. In his book *Alice in Wonderland,* Humpty Dumpty said: "When I use a word it means just what I choose it to mean."

6. Comparisons

This is often a very effective type of specific to use in a speech. A comparison presents characteristics, features, or qualities which are similar. Often it may show an audience a connection between what they know and what they don't know. Or a comparison may state a relationship which is a surprise.

The Governor of Puerto Rico, Carlos Romer–Barcello, included this comparison in a speech:

Puerto Rico remains poor today, by comparison with the United States as a whole. Our per capita income is only about half that of Mississippi, the poorest state in the nation.

In a speech presented in London, the Prime Minister of Great Britain, Margaret Thatcher, made this comparison:

Governor Reagan's victory, like the successes of Britain's overseas policy in the last year, leaves us, I believe, in good shape to cope with the storms that lie ahead.

7. Contrasts

They present, as you know, differences.
Former President Kennedy presented in his inaugural address a contrast which has become so famous it's almost a popular folk-saying:

Ask not what your country can do for you; ask what you can do for your country.

(However, those words were quite close to a line written way back in 1864 by Oliver Wendell Holmes, Jr.)
Liz Carpenter, a writer who had been executive as-

sistant to former President Johnson, included this contrast in a recent speech:

> In 1960, there were three and a half million college students in this country. Today there are twelve million—more than half are women and many minorities are among them.

A speech presented by Barry Goldwater, Senator from Arizona, included this interesting contrast:

> In Japan, twenty percent of all bachelor's degrees and forty percent of all master's degrees are in engineering; in the United States, only five percent of each category are engineering degrees.

8. Audiovisual Aids

You've heard the Chinese proverb, "One picture is worth a thousand words." If that's true, then a picture is worth about eight minutes of a speech—most of us speak at about 125 words a minute.

Audiovisual aids can help improve your speeches by:

1. Centering the attention of your listeners.
2. Adding interest to what you say.
3. Making your ideas easier to understand.
4. Emphasizing your information and ideas.
5. Helping your listeners to remember your talk.

Those benefits have been proven by studies made across the nation, brought together largely by researchers at the University of Southern California. They say: Use visual aids to help get your ideas across in your speeches.

Visual aids can be as simple as a few words on a chalkboard. Or, they can be very complex electronic mixtures of television, films, slides, and more.

Sometimes visuals are projected on three or more screens all at the same time. They're called *multimedia presentations.* Projectors are behind the screens, rather than behind the audience, so lights in the auditorium can be kept on while listeners take notes.

In some special lecture halls a dozen or more projectors are used. Controls are built into the lectern. The speaker flips switches, turns knobs, and different audiovisual aids appear. More complex installations have the controls preprogramed in electronic memory units. They automatically turn on one projector, turn another off, for example, at just the right moment in a speech.

A speech in such a hall goes like this. A speaker will show an outline of his talk on a screen on one side, using an overhead projector. On another screen he'll project a film clip of his topic in action. On still another screen, he'll flash key questions—"Can you spot what makes this work?" And over all those visuals, the speaker will be talking away, explaining the subject.

Well, your speeches certainly don't have to be that complex.

To start with, consider showing your listeners a few key words or simple drawings on a *chalkboard.* "Chalkboard" is today's word for what used to be called a blackboard. Now these boards come in green, brown, even white—you write on them with colored chalk.

Or, put the information you want in a visual on a piece of *cardboard.* It can be a graph, chart, diagram, map, a list of points—there are many possibilities.

Another simple visual aid: a *flip chart.* That's a pad of paper, usually about three-by-four feet. There are special easels to hold a flip chart. Or you can just prop it up against the front wall where you're talking. Then you can turn the pages and show visuals you've drawn out ahead of time. Or, you can write on the flip chart as you give your speech.

If you want to move up a bit, try an *overhead projector.* Many places in which speeches are given now have them—hotel conference rooms, classrooms, meeting rooms at churches, and such. Overhead projectors are easy to use and can make quite an impression on your audience.

The overhead projector is placed right at the speaker's location. You write with a felt-point pen on the top—the desk-like—part of the projector. You face the audience; you don't have to turn your back on your listeners to do your writing. You can use a variety of colors. What you write is projected on a screen behind you. You can have drawings made up ahead of time. Preparing them is fast, easy, inexpensive. If you have access to almost any kind of photocopy machine, you can make really impressive presentations. You can project color photos from magazines. You can show small charts from a newspaper, for example, making them big enough to be seen by a large audience. You can use a great variety of printed materials as visuals in your speeches.

Slides, films, recordings, video recordings (TV recordings) all make effective aids for your speeches.

But there are some real hazards in using audiovisual aids in your speeches.

1. Aids might not be appropriate for the speaking situation. Don't bring in an array of visuals for a five-minute talk on the need to vote at tomorrow's election. On the other hand, if you're giving a speech to teenagers about safe driving, you'd better use visuals because many of those kids think they've already heard all there is to know about driving a car.

2. Audiovisual aids can chew up a lot of your time as you select and prepare them. Decide if your speech would be better if you worked more on the content, the structure, and the delivery.

3. You need to practice using your aids! That's one of the biggest jams speakers get into—having visuals ready, but failing to figure out ahead of time how to turn on the projector. Or having a pen that won't write on the overhead projector. Or not bringing an extension cord for the slide projector. Or . . . the hazards are many. Practice!

4. Finally, you must make sure your aids work. When TV was broadcasting live programs—before the

days of videotape—one announcer was trying to show how easy a can opener worked, only to find that he had a faulty one as millions of people watched him struggle! Check your aids. Check them several times, *before* you give your speech.

Those, then, are the types of information you can use in your speeches. But where do you get that material?

The most important source, remember, is your own mind—what you already know about the subject.

Turn next to whatever magazines or books you may have. Look at ones which may be available in your shop or office.

Talk to your friends. You may be surprised at what they know about the subject of your speech. Or, they may tell you such things as, "I know a guy at our church who collects books about that subject."

One of your very best sources is the Reference Librarian at your local library. Many public libraries have such specialists. Your nearby college or university may also have someone assigned to help dig out bits of information. But be fair to them. Ask them for answers to just brief, specific questions. Don't phone up and ask, "What information have you got on raising dahlias?" For that, you should go to the library yourself. But if you're at home or in your office, planning your speech, and you find you need to know when dahlias were first raised in the United States, then you have a legitimate question to ask your librarian by phone.

In fact, a good Reference Librarian can be your best assistant in preparing your speeches. If you give speeches fairly often, it would be worth your time to go to your library and meet the Reference Librarian in person. Generally, he or she is someone who enjoys digging out obscure bits of information. Such specialists get a kick out of finding out the real name of that famous movie star, or the cost of our first aircraft carrier, or how high in the sky those satellites are that relay our TV programs.

So now you've gathered together the ideas and the information you want to present in your speech. But they're mostly a stack of jumbled notes. A lot of specifics in no particular order. It's time to organize your material—to put the content of your speech in a clear, specific, easy-to-understand structure.

CHECKPOINTS:
GATHER YOUR IDEAS AND INFORMATION

Check off each of the following points to help insure you do a good job gathering material for your speeches.

_____ 1. Don't start by going to a library or other such source.

_____ 2. Begin by jotting down notes of what you already know.

_____ 3. Use information—specifics—to:

    _____ (1) Prove your ideas, points.

    _____ (2) Clarify your points.

    _____ (3) Make points memorable.

    _____ (4) Add interest to your speech.

_____ 4. Use a variety of information:

    _____ (1) Examples

    _____ (2) Quotations

    _____ (3) Statistics

    _____ (4) Stories

    _____ (5) Definitions

    _____ (6) Comparisons

    _____ (7) Contrasts

    _____ (8) Audiovisual aids

_____ 5. NOW, if you're still short of information, go to your library or other sources.

_____ 6. Get to know your local Reference Librarian.

6

STEP #4: Organize Your Material

> *Mend your speech a little,*
> *lest it may mar your fortunes.*
> SHAKESPEARE

ONE OF THE BEST-KEPT SECRETS of successful professional speakers is this:

> *Get your speech organized very clearly—in a few very specific, precise points—and it's much more likely that your audience will get your message.*

Failure to know—or use—that secret is usually the main reason so many speeches are forgotten so quickly.

A speech MUST be designed in a structure that's easy-to-follow, *if* it's to achieve its purpose—to get your listeners to accept your ideas, remember what you say, and take the action you want.

In the language of the 1950s, "You've got to get organized!" Or, to use one of the pop phrases of the early 1980s, "Get your act together!"

To get your speech together, all you have to do is apply the following simple *format*. The format is a general guide or pattern for the design of a speech.

Any speech. The same format can be used for a talk on any topic, at any speaking occasion, for any speaking situation, whether you're giving a short, casual talk to a troop of Boy Scouts or presenting a formal appeal to a committee of your state legislature.

Here's that all-purpose—all-speech—format:

FORMAT FOR A SPEECH

    I. Introduction
       A. Attention-getter
       B. Preview
    II. Discussion
       A. Main points
       B. Arranged logically
       C. Supported with data
    III. Conclusion
       A. Review
       B. Memorable statement

Take a moment to really study that format. It consists of just fifteen words, yet it's *the essential key* to your designing an effective speech.

Note that the format includes three *main parts* to a speech—the introduction, the discussion, and the conclusion. In this step of your speech preparation, you'll get tips on how to prepare the discussion part of your speech.

There are two very good reasons for designing the discussion first, leaving the introduction and the conclusion until later.

First, the discussion contains most of the content of your speech. As a general guide, the length of a speech usually breaks down to be about:

15% for the Introduction
75% for the Discussion
10% for the Conclusion

Thus, for a typical twenty-minute speech, the time you'll have for each main part of a speech would be about:

3 minutes for the Introduction
15 minutes for the Discussion
2 minutes for the Conclusion

Or consider a five-minute talk. That's all the time you're allowed at many public meetings, such as presenting an appeal to your city council. The typical introduction of a speaker, announcement of an event, and many other speeches of today are often briefer. The time you have for each part of a five-minute talk is:

45 seconds for the Introduction
3 minutes and 45 seconds for the Discussion
sion
30 seconds for the Conclusion

"Not much time!" you say? Think of those TV commercials that bombard us constantly. Very few are longer than sixty seconds. Many are just thirty seconds long, some twenty seconds, some only ten seconds. They even telecast a few eight-second and even three-second bullets. Yet extensive million-dollar campaigns are carried by such brief messages.

The trick is, of course, to organize your commercial —your speech—so clearly that you'll communicate your message in only as many words as you really need.

Still, those time guides for the length of a speech are just that—guides. Speakers do make exceptions. For years in California, highway patrolmen have been speaking to groups of high-school students about safe driving. Now what can you tell a high-school kid about safe driving??? Just about every new driver thinks his driving skills are perfect! So those patrolmen talk to audiences which are mighty *un*interested in those speeches. To get those audiences listening, the patrolmen often spend more than half of a speech on just the attention-getter—the first part of the introduction to a speech. They begin, often, with a humorous story about a traffic stop. They'll then follow with more stories—some humorous, some tragic, some that happened locally, others from throughout the state. Finally they reach the main point of their talks—very brief discussions of just two or so tips on safe driving. Then they conclude with maybe just one more brief, pointed story, and are finished. The introduction to their talks is often as much as eighty percent of a total speech; the discussion perhaps just fifteen percent; the conclusion a mere five percent.

The point: While those time guides to the length of a speech work for most speeches, you may have to adjust them in special speaking situations.

The **second reason** you should plan the discussion part of your speech before you plan the introduction and the conclusion is that it's much easier.

Note that the format states that the first words of your speech should present an attention-getter. That's a statement that will instantly grab the interest of your listeners. But it's hard to begin planning a speech by first dreaming up a really sparkling, stimulating opening. It's much easier to go ahead with the design of the rest of your speech—the discussion—while keeping alert to finding that fascinating bit you need to open your speech. As you work on your speech, you'll come across a really good attention-getting story, or startling statistic, or some other great opener. Then you just move it from whatever point it may relate to in the discussion part of your speech, and place it right up there at the beginning of your talk, as your very first statement. Whammo! You've got your audience listening! They're not mentally drifting off as you plod through a lot of dull stuff like: "Sure glad to be speaking to you today." Instead, right off, you got them *with* you!

So how do you organize the discussion part of your speeches?

First, you need to decide what form you're going to use as you write down the ideas and information you'll present in your speech. You have three options:

1. A full script
2. An outline
3. Notes

Don't try a script. Writing your speeches out word-for-word takes much more time and effort. And delivering a speech from a script is difficult. Most of us have a writing style which is very different from our style of speaking. We use more formal words and sentences when we write. A speech should be closer to conversation than to written expression.

Most speakers find it best—by far—to prepare an outline of what they want to say in a speech. The outline doesn't have to be formal. Full sentences are not needed. Rather, jot down just enough words so you'll be able to recall quickly and clearly the points you want to present.

Avoid general statements in an outline. If you're giving a speech explaining why a project is running late, don't write your outline in a broad term such as "Causes." Rather, name each cause—"Not enough time for planning," "Two-week strike by carpenters," and such. When you outline your facts, don't write generalizations such as "costs." Instead, write down the specific figures—"$5,000 above estimates for the foundation," for example.

Here's a sample of an outline for a talk to a city council.

```
  I. INTRODUCTION
     A. In a city that's launched a
        score of costly and wasteful
        projects in the last decade,
        we're now about to start the
        worst of all!
     B. The widening of Monty Street
        should be stopped--for three
        specific reasons.
 II. DISCUSSION
     A. Costs too much--$9.1
        million!
        1. That's more than our
```

           state capital spent on
           all its streets for the
           entire last year--and
           that's a city five times
           larger than our town.

     2. The cost comes to more
        than $1.5 million for
        each of the six short
        blocks to be widened.

B. Not needed.
     1. The present accident rate
        is no higher than any
        six-block stretch in our
        town's quietest resi-
        dential area.
     2. The present flow of
        traffic is always at the
        twenty-five-mile-per-hour
        speed limit except for
        less than four percent of
        the time.
        a. Weekday traffic moves
           slowly for only about
           twenty minutes each
           morning and afternoon.
        b. Weekend traffic slows
           for brief periods
           totaling only about
           two hours a day--
           mostly by sight-seeing
           tourists who want to
           slow.

C. Solves no problems.
     1. The traffic bottleneck:
        will simply be moved six
        blocks down the street.
     2. The area's appearance:

```
               The street itself will
               look better, but the
               major visual mess--the
               buildings along the
               road--will still be
               unsightly.
            3. There are no other
               problems involved!
   III. CONCLUSION
         A. The widening of Monty Street
            costs too much, is not
            needed, and solves no
            problems.
         B. The widening of Monty Street
            should be stopped--now!
```

After completing an outline of a speech, some speakers then prepare note cards to use while they speak. Others prefer to skip the outline. They find it easier to prepare note cards as they plan their speeches. Then they use those same notes to refer to while speaking.

Either way, your note cards, too, should be specific. When you're standing up there before an audience, trying to remember what to say next, you don't want to look at your note card and find that the next point you've written down is simply "Future." In the pressure of presenting the speech, that one word may not be enough to remind you just what you wanted to say about the future. Again be specific. Brief, but specific.

A few more tips about your note cards: Write on just one side of a card. Then you won't have a chance of getting confused while you speak, trying to figure out which side of a card has your next point. And write your notes large enough so you won't have any trouble seeing them, even if stage lights are shining in your eyes or there are other distractions. It's far better to use several cards, rather than trying to crowd an entire speech on one card, using tiny writing. Finally, number your cards clearly, to help make sure you keep them in sequence.

A note card for the speech outlined above would look like this:

I. INTRODUCTION
   A. A score of costly, wasteful projects in past decade, now another!
   B. Widening Monty St--NO!
II. DISCUSSION
   A. Too costly--$9.1 mil.
     1. More than capital spend last year, & it 5 times larger
     2. More than $1.5 mil. per block
   B. Not needed
     1. Accident rate same as residential 6 blocks
     2. Traffic flows at limit-- except:
       a. Weekdays: 20 min., morn & eve
       b. Weekends: 2 hrs. by sight-seers
   C. Solves no problems
     1. Bottleneck: moves just 6 blocks
     2. Appearance: buildings will still be mess
     3. No other problems!
III. CONCLUSION
   A. Costs too much, not needed, solves no problems
   B. Vote no!

Next, remember our *Format for a Speech*. Start with

the first item in the discussion part of the speech—the item underlined in the following excerpt from that format—*main points*.

II. Discussion
    A. Main points
    B. Arranged logically
    C. Supported with data

Begin by making a list—a long list—of the points you *might* present in your speech. The list should include a dozen or so points. Then you'll have plenty from which to select. Jot down every point which comes to mind. The first ones might not be the best. So take time to make a long list to help insure you'll include all of the significant points you'll want to present. Then cut that list down to the two-to-five best points.

Many listeners are not able to remember more than five points. And if you present just one point, you're basing all your sell on just one pitch. If your listeners do not accept that one point, they may reject your entire presentation. It's much safer to give your listeners at least two points to consider. Then if they doubt one, they still may accept your basic idea.

Your main points should not be confused with your facts. Facts, remember, are the statistics, quotations, and such which support your points—prove them, clarify them, make them memorable and more interesting.

Suppose you are to give a speech to your club to urge members to help in a drive for new members. The points of your speech might include:

A. Our membership is falling.
B. Other clubs have more members.
C. New members will provide us with more help on our work projects.

Those are valid points which you've decided that the

available information supports. That information might include:

1. We now have 40 members—last year we had 62.
2. The average membership in other branches of our club is around 75 members.
3. We do 6 projects a year, and every one of us has to work on every project.

You'll need additional bits of information, too, for your full speech, but that's enough for this example. We've shown the difference between your main points —which we're working with now—and your information, your facts and data and such, which we'll deal with later.

Your next task in preparing your speech is to attend to that second point in the discussion part of your speech format:

II. Discussion
  A. Main points
  <u>B. Arranged logically</u>
  C. Supported with data

Now you have to *sequence your points*—put them in the most logical, effective order possible. That's valuable to help make sure listeners will be more likely to accept your ideas and remember them.

This is one of the most important steps in planning a speech. Arrange your points clearly and you've greatly increased the chances that your speech will be successful.

To arrange the main points in your speech, there are four main patterns you can use. They are:

1. Time
2. Space
3. Topic
4. Problem–solution

Which pattern is best? Depends on your speaking situation. And the impact you want to make on your listeners. And the information you have to present. And . . . well, you get the idea. Picking the pattern for your speech is another one of the steps in which you have to apply your best judgment based on that analysis you made back in Step #2—that analysis of your speaking situation, the occasion on which you're speaking and yourself as a speaker.

Here's how you can use those patterns to present your ideas and information effectively in your speeches.

1. Time Pattern

This is the pattern that usually works best if you're talking about how to do something, or about an activity, an historic event, or such.

If you're talking about how to plan a trip, you could organize your ideas and information into these main points:

A. Planning before you leave
B. Planning during the trip
C. Planning after the trip

Under that first point—planning before you leave— you might present facts about how to gather information, how to work with a travel agent, how to budget, and such. To support that second point—planning during the trip—you could talk about how to plan for changes that may come up in your schedule, or how to plan side trips that you might find interesting. For the third point—planning after the trip—you might offer tips on how to take care of those credit card charges that keep coming in for months, and how to use what you learned on this trip to improve your next one.

By putting all those tips on planning a trip into a logical order, your listeners are much more likely to remember them.

Here's another example of use of a time pattern—

for a speech about unrest in America. Your points might be:

A. In the 1950s, threats from internal and external sources
B. In the 1960s, a lingering war
C. In the 1970s, demonstrations
D. In the 1980s, what can we expect?

To be most effective, a time pattern should present your points in the sequence in which they happen. For example, an *in*effective use of a time pattern would be this order of points in a speech about tips on typing:

A. Be sure paper is in typewriter straight
B. Erase carefully
C. Insert paper without mussing it
D. Line up margins exactly

Clearly, those points are *not* in the order that a typist should do them. Being out of sequence, they'll be harder for the audience to follow.

To make sure you're using a time pattern effectively, ask yourself:

1. Do the points in my speech consist of units of time?
2. Are they equal or comparable time units?
3. Are they logical?
4. Are they the best sequence of points for this speech?

If you have to say no to any one of those questions, try this pattern:

2. Space Pattern

In this pattern, you organize the points of your speech on the basis of some physical or geographic sequence.

If you're talking about the tax problems in your state, you might organize your ideas this way:

A. Tax problems of coastal towns
B. Tax problems of farm communities
C. Tax problems of major cities

Those points illustrate another major advantage of picking a particular pattern for the design of your speech. Once you start sequencing your material, you often discover either one of two problems.

One: You might be trying to cover far too much material. The solution: cut. Limit your topic. In that example about tax problems, maybe you should talk just about the coastal towns. Or about the farm communities only. Maybe you should concentrate on the cities alone.

Your second possible problem: You might not really have enough to talk about. That is often revealed as you start trying to fit your material into some pattern. You might find you actually have just one point. What should you do? Either dig out more material, or expand your topic into related information. The decision, again, depends entirely on just what *purpose* you have in mind for your speech.

Here's another application of a space pattern:

A. Amateur radio activities in America
B. Amateur radio activities in Europe
C. Amateur radio activities in Asia

Using a space pattern like that will keep your speech from jumping around. You'll avoid using a story about amateur radio activity in California, then an example from Japan, followed by some statistics from the U.S. government—to mention just a few of the specific facts such a speech might include.

However, keep those main points in logical, sensible order. For example, consider these main points from a speech a student gave in one of my classes. His topic: How to buy a car.

A. What to look for on the dashboard
B. Choosing the color
C. Important features of the trunk
D. How to check the motor

That's a kind of space pattern in that the points do present different parts—locations—related to a car. But of course you can see that they are not in a logical sequence. They're not in the order we'd consider them. And they are not equal parts of the topic.

To check your use of a space pattern, ask yourself:

1. Are these points logical?
2. Are they about equal space units?
3. Do they present my ideas in the best possible order?

If not, consider using:

3. Topic Pattern

Ahh—you'll love this one! It will fit any subject. It's effective in any speaking situation. It's used more than any other pattern.

Sometimes it's called the "catch-all" pattern. If your ideas and information don't seem to fit into some other pattern, use the topic pattern.

Here are some examples. For a speech about the joys of sailing, your points might be:

A. The lure of the open sea
B. Relaxation at its best
C. A real change of pace

For a talk about your concerns about your child's school, a topic pattern could include these points:

A. Insufficient concern by teachers
B. Dangerous playground equipment
C. Lack of planning

You may have already started to spot some of the problems speakers have when they use the topic pattern. The points often lack focus. Under point A, "Insufficient concern by teachers," you could talk about teachers who don't grade homework, teachers who don't communicate effectively, teachers who aren't motivating the gifted youngsters, teachers who . . . Well, you get the idea. Speeches can easily become too long, trying to cover far too much material, when you use a topic pattern.

Furthermore, the topic pattern doesn't allow you to be very creative. All you do is present a series of statements, following each with your information. Often, the points don't have much relationship to each other. Sometimes the logic in a topic pattern is harder to follow. The result: Many listeners seem to forget these speeches faster.

Still, the topic pattern is a good one because it gives the speaker so much flexibility. Whatever your subject, it will fit into the topic pattern. And it is at least better to use it than to simply wander through your material.

But there's one more pattern you might use. However, it's used *in*effectively more than any other.

4. Problem–solution Pattern

This one's useful when you're proposing a change. Or trying to get something improved, offering a new idea, or recommending a plan of action.

A well-constructed problem–solution pattern can be very effective indeed. It presents your ideas in a very logical, very clear sequence.

Suppose you're giving a talk to your planning commission on the need for a stop sign at a dangerous corner in town. You could organize your recommendation this way:

A. Problem: This is a dangerous intersection.
    1. Been more wrecks here than at any other local corner in the past year.

    2. Speeding cars can be seen any time of the day.
B. Solution: Install a stop sign.
    1. It will direct the flow of traffic.
    2. It will make speeders stop at this corner.

Notice the careful balance of points in that partial outline for a speech. The problem is stated specifically. It's followed by two precise summations of why it's dangerous. (The full speech would then present specific data, such as the number of wrecks at the corner, followed by the number at the next most dangerous corner; then more data documenting your statement about speeding cars; and whatever other information might support those points.)

The solution in that example is also well-balanced— it presents two logical benefits or values in installing a stop sign.

Most important: Note that the first part of the problem—"more wrecks"—would indeed be eased by the first part of the solution—"direct the flow of traffic." And the second part of the problem is, similarly, solved by the second point in the solution.

Contrast that effective problem–solution pattern with this *illogical* one:

A. Problem: Our marina is falling apart.
    1. Not enough berths.
    2. Poor service.
B. Solution: Need more staff.
    1. They'll keep area clean.
    2. They'll speed repairs.

Hope you've spotted the several illogical points in that partial outline. The statement of the problem— that the "marina is falling apart"—is not followed by statements which show that it is indeed "falling apart." Rather, the two points which follow are unrelated to the problem—"not enough berths" and "poor service" don't at all show that the marina is "falling apart." Next, the solution—"need more staff"—won't provide the additional berths the speaker says are needed. And that additional staff won't necessarily solve the problem of "poor service"—what might more likely be needed is more training of the present staff so they'll no longer provide "poor service."

Well, there are other inconsistencies in that example, too, but you've probably spotted them. Still, don't scoff at that poor use of a problem–solution pattern. I actually heard that speech in a public meeting.

In sum: In using a problem–solution pattern, be sure that the solution you propose does in fact solve the problem you're identifying. Or, if you're in a debate or other adversary situation, having to give a speech against someone offering a solution, listen carefully to that speaker's proposal. Very often the solution is but a different way of doing something, or the addition of more staff or more equipment or more paperwork—not at all necessarily solutions as is so often claimed.

So now you've got the points of your speech pinpointed, and you've got them in some kind of pattern. You have just one more task to complete the planning of the discussion part of your speech. It's time to attend to that third step in structuring the discussion part of our speech format:

II. Discussion
   A. Main points
   B. Arranged logically
   C. Supported with data

You gathered that data in the last step—the previous chapter. You should now have a good stack of stories, statistics, examples, quotations—remember the eight different types of data?

Now you simply line up that information under each of the main points of your speech. Try to *distribute* the information evenly. Don't use eight facts to support one point. That much information for one point may overload the memories of your listeners. Furthermore, if you use too much data for one point, some in your audience may get suspicious—they may wonder: Why is the speaker trying to prove that statement so strongly?— Is there something hidden behind all those figures?

On the other hand, don't support a point with just one bit of data. Then some listeners may think you don't have much of a case. And if some people doubt that single fact you've presented, then you've probably lost your chance to get them to accept the point that fact supports. Even worse, if you use just one fact and someone points out any error at all in it—even a very slight error—many listeners will reject your point completely.

So it's best to use, say, three or four facts to support each of your points. Then you'll have a more solid base on which to validate your points.

You should also use a *variety* of information. Don't use statistics only. They can become boring. Besides, some people don't trust statistics. They may be more impressed with examples. But a speech of examples only may lose your listeners who are more open to comparisons with other situations, for example. Therefore, use as many of the eight different types of information as you can. Mix quotations, definitions, contrasts, statistics, all the types of data into your speech.

Now you've got most of your speech together. It's time to plan what you're going to say to open your speech—the introduction.

CHECKPOINTS:
ORGANIZE YOUR MATERIAL

As you plan your speeches, use this list of checkpoints to help structure your material.

_____ 1. Follow this:

FORMAT FOR A SPEECH

_____ I. Introduction
_____ A. Attention-getter
_____ B. Preview
_____ II. Discussion
_____ A. Main points
_____ B. Arranged logically
_____ C. Supported with data
_____ III. Conclusion
_____ A. Review
_____ B. Memorable statement

_____ 2. Follow, usually, these guides for the lengths of each part of your speeches:
_____ 15% for the Introduction
_____ 75% for the Discussion
_____ 10% for the Conclusion
_____ 3. Prepare an outline and/or note cards
_____ 4. Arrange your information logically, using one of these patterns:
_____ (1) Time
_____ (2) Space
_____ (3) Topic
_____ (4) Problem–Solution

7

STEP #5: Plan the Beginning of Your Speech

> *Speech is a mirror of the soul:*
> *as a man speaks, so is he.*
>
> PUBLILIUS SYRUS

WHY DO SO many TV commercials begin with a glimpse of a strikingly pretty girl? Why do many ads show the product being used by a macho male? Why do travel brochures often feature a couple in skimpy swim suits?

Of course you know the answer. They're trying to get your attention.

In designing a speech, that should be the intent of your very first statement. Remember our basic structure:

FORMAT FOR A SPEECH

    I. Introduction

        A. Attention-getter

        B. Preview

You might feel that you should open your speech with

a greeting—to the chairman, the audience, to distinguished guests, possibly to others. Do so if you must, but be as brief as you can. Many listeners do not tune in to a speaker until after the welcoming remarks. Many in your audience will continue to look around the room, think about the last speaker, wonder what they're going to do after your speech, figure out how to get across the hall to say "hello" to that guy they'd not seen for a while.

Therefore, the best speakers find it most effective to present an attention-getter first. Then they express any necessary greetings after they've captured the attention of the audience.

To put it another way, *to get your audience's attention should be the first and total purpose of the opening words of your speech.*

President Reagan emphasized his attention-getters in one speech by saying:

Let me just give a few "attention-getters" from the audit. The federal budget is out of control and we face runaway deficits of almost $80 billion for this budget year that ends September 30. That deficit is larger than the entire federal budget in 1957 and so is the almost $80 billion we will pay in interest this year on the national debt.

The President used the first of the ten main types of attention-getters you can use to get your audiences listening to you:

1. Stating a startling fact
2. Asking a question
3. Telling a joke
4. Presenting a quotation
5. Giving an example, illustration, or story
6. Referring to the occasion
7. Pointing to an historic event
8. Complimenting the audience
9. Using a gimmick
10. Emphasizing the importance of the subject

Here are some examples and tips for using each of those techniques.

1. Stating a startling fact

The power of unusual facts is illustrated by the syndicated column called "The Grab Bag," written by L. M. Boyd. It appears regularly in newspapers throughout the nation. It consists of nothing but a couple of dozen unrelated, uncommon facts. "Ketchup 150 years ago hereabouts was a patent medicine." "Four out of five mothers cradle their infants in their left arm." "Polls show ninety-seven percent of the university students don't know the words to their school songs."

You could use such facts as attention-getters in your speeches. The one about ketchup might introduce a speech about today's federal controls on medicines. Or a speech about how times change. Or . . . well, you can figure out other subjects which it and those other facts might lead into.

Finding such facts is not at all as difficult as might be thought. You can of course read Boyd's columns. Or you can skim encyclopedias or search through your daily newspaper. Those sources will give you random facts that you then need to somehow tie in with your speech subject.

But it's far easier to keep alert for unusual facts as you gather your information for your speech. If you're preparing a talk about the need for a high school course on family problems, you might come across the fact (true!) that during a typical recent year there were fifteen boys in Hawaii who had been divorced while only fourteen years of age. Grab that fact out of your pile of data, move it up to the first sentence of your speech, and you have a pretty powerful attention-getter.

2. Asking a question

This is one of the easiest techniques to use. There is always something you can ask your audience about the subject of your speech.

Are you unhappy with the amount of taxes you pay?

If a visitor from abroad asked you what should be seen in your town, what would you reply?

Do you wonder what causes the many changes in our society today?

But some questions may not be effective attention-getters. Consider these:

Do you know the name of the richest country in the world?

How long has it been since you've checked your insurance policies?

Have you ever noticed how many people wear braided belts?

What might some of your listeners respond—mentally—to those questions? The richest country? Some may think, *With my budget problems, who cares?* Checked your insurance? Some listeners may think, *Whoops, here comes another sales pitch!* Noticed braided belts? *Who would bother about such a detail?*

Such negative reactions to your opening question will make it harder for you to get your audience thinking with you. To be effective, your opening question should get your listeners thinking positively. They should be stimulated, wanting to hear more of what you've got to say.

Questions which get listeners involved with your speech are most effective. Try to get them to listen actively—to think along with you. I've heard speakers get audiences with them by asking such questions as:

If you could—or had to—live the rest of your life in another country, which would you select?

What's the one thing you own that you could absolutely not do without?

How long has it been since you've listened to nature? Heard a bird sing? Heard the wind move? Heard leaves rustle?

3. Telling a joke

Many speakers find that the ideas they present in their speeches are accepted more readily when their audiences are put in a jovial mood. So they open their speeches by telling a joke.

Jokes which bring big laughs when heard from the mouth of Johnny Carson, for example, often don't come through as funny when they appear in print. So rather than giving you examples, you're left to your own storehouse of humor to illustrate these tips on how to use jokes effectively.

But don't feel that your speeches must include jokes. Some of us aren't good at telling jokes. Others feel that using humor just isn't their style. A joke poorly told can backfire—help the audience lose confidence in you as a speaker. And, of course, many speech subjects are not suitable for jokes.

A basic guide is to be sure your jokes have some logical relationship to your speeches. We've all heard speakers who begin speeches with such lines as, "Let me tell you this really funny story I heard just the other day. It doesn't have anything to do with my speech, but I think you'll get a laugh!"

The point is that everything you say in your speech should, of course, relate directly to the subject of your speech. If you can't find a joke that fits, don't use one.

Still, there are a couple of tricks you can use to make many jokes fit many speech subjects.

One technique is the *switch*. Comedians sometimes

call this "changing the peg." That means changing the setting, characters, or subject of the joke.

Suppose you are to give a speech about off-shore oil pollution. You hear a good joke about backpacking. That doesn't seem to tie in with your speech subject. So try changing the gag from backpacking to a walk on the beach. Then you should be able to connect the joke directly with your speech subject.

Another way to tie a joke to your speech subject is through a *transition*. That's a phrase, sentence, occasionally a couple of sentences which link the point of your joke to the point of your speech. Johnny Carson uses transitions often, and effectively, in his opening monologues. He relates one joke to the next with such lines as:

Well, what else is in the news today?

Oh, did you see the TV report on? . . .

Say, remember the other day when someone said . . .

Speakers use transitions to connect a joke with the subjects of their speeches when they say, for example:

Well, we can all laugh at this person's problems, but think about how you would handle the problem of . . .

I'm glad you got a good laugh out of that story, because it may help you as we consider for a few minutes the serious implications of . . .

In addition, humor used to open speeches should usually be short and to the point. Many of the well-known "shaggy dog stories," for example, are so long that many listeners become impatient and start to think, *Come on, when is this speaker going to get to the point of his speech?*

Finally, the appropriateness of a joke should be considered carefully. It often helps to personalize a joke by adding names. Rather than saying "A couple of guys were, . . ." you might add names such as "Pat and Mike were . . ." But then you run the danger of developing resentment, perhaps even anger, from the Pats and Mikes in your audience, and perhaps you'll antagonize their friends, too, plus possibly all the Irish whom those two names are often taken to represent.

The point: Study every joke you're thinking about using to make sure it will not offend someone and thereby detract from the success of your speech.

4. Presenting a quotation

Back in Step #3, Gather Your Ideas and Information, you got some tips on using quotations as one form of information to support the points you present in your speeches.

You can find quotations, you'll remember, in a variety of reference books. Or you can collect them as you gather material for your speeches.

Quotations are a good way to open a speech—to get the attention of your listeners—because people like to hear what others have said about the subject of your speech.

Sometimes it's effective to open a speech with a quotation made years ago about the subject of your speech. You may be giving a talk on the fairness of a new law, for example, and begin by saying:

Way back around 2,100 B.C.—nearly 4,000 years ago!—Hammurabi, the greatest king of the first Babylonian dynasty, said, 'If a man destroy the eye of another man, they shall destroy his eye.' Today, our laws often follow that same centuries-old principle . . .

But remember the one big weakness in using a quotation. With a little digging, someone can almost always find another quote that says just the opposite of the quote you've used. Often the source of that conflicting quotation is every bit as important, knowledgeable, or respected as the person you've quoted. But then, chances are rare that someone in your audience will be able to remember an opposing quote at the very moment you start your speech.

Then there are some quotes which can be used to open a speech on almost any subject. One is this gem by Lord Macaulay, English statesman of the 1800s:

> Men are never so likely to settle a question rightly as when they discuss it freely.

You could then go on to say something such as:

> Well, we here this evening can be expected to find the right solution to this problem, because by our very speaking we are indeed following Lord Macaulay's advice—we are discussing this problem freely.

However, in using such quotes be sure you're not stretching too far the tie-in between it and your speech subject. That might get your listeners thinking negatively again—and that's the main reaction you want to *avoid* as you begin to speak.

5. Giving an example, illustration, or story

At a management seminar in Stockholm, Loet Velmans, chairman of Hill and Kowlton Inc., began his speech by saying:

> There seems to be something in the human psyche that makes years ending in nine or in zero important. In the nine-ending years, we tend to look back and assess where we have been. In the zero-ending years, we tend to look forward to see where we're going. Both are fascinating exercises and both assume that there is something magical about an artificial construction called a decade. But the future *is* important.

His example led clearly, directly, to his statement of the subject of his speech. That's one of the main advantages of beginning a speech with an example, illustration, or story.

Another advantage is that stories about people in particular are especially effective openers for speeches. Again, people like to hear about people. Don't you find yourself getting caught up in the following opening to a speech?

Last Sunday two teenagers went for a sail on Monterey Bay. One was deaf. The other was wearing leg braces—a victim of polio. Suddenly their boat . . .

Where do you find examples, illustrations, stories to use as attention-getters to start your speeches? Again, go through the information you have available for your talk, then pick out from it a dramatic story, a sparkling illustration, a mind-grabbing example.

And if you can't find one? Then try opening your speech by:

6. Referring to the occasion

The chairman of the Federal Maritime Commission, Leslie Kanuk, used this technique in one of his speeches by stating:

This is National Transportation Week, a week during which all Americans take recognition of transportation's importance to our defense, our economy, and our way of life.

The Ambassador of Panama to the United States, Juan José Amado III, used the same type of opening when he said:

Just over a year ago, the first phase in the process of reverting back to Panama the land and facilities of the so-called "Canal Zone" began.

You can use this same technique by beginning your speech with a statement of the reason for the meeting, for example. Or, tell the audience what problem, event, or such brought about the meeting at which you're speaking.

While this opening is usually not very dramatic or stimulating, it does have the advantage of letting you emphasize the reason you're speaking. You can point to the mutual interest or subject that brought you and the audience together for your speech.

7. Pointing to an historic event

Every day of the year has been the occasion of at least several varied—often quite interesting—events. Many newspapers publish a short column entitled "Today's Almanac." For October 20, for example, the column listed, among other events:

Today is the 294th day of the year, with 72 days to come.

1977: first takeoff by supersonic Concorde airliner from New York's Kennedy Airport.

1968: Mrs. Jacqueline Kennedy married Aristotle Onassis, the Greek shipping magnate.

1964: former President Hoover died, aged 90.

1944: American troops started recapture of the Philippines from the Japanese.

1918: Germany accepted terms to end World War I.

1859: educator John Dewey was born.

One or more of these events may relate directly or indirectly to the subject of your speech.

Consider that event for the year 1964, the death of former President Hoover. It could be used to introduce such varied subjects as:

The adequacy of services for the aged.

Graduates: Are you ready for leadership?

Is early retirement wasting too much of our productive years?

Can America be run from Washington today?

How can this community get national leaders to act on our problems?

Other sources for finding out what happened in history on the day you speak include *Dictionary of Dates* by Robert Collison, *Anniversaries and Holidays* by Ruth W. Gregory, and *The American Book of Days* by Jane M. Match. You can usually find all of those books in your local library.

8. Complimenting the audience

This can be a good opener for a speech because we all love to be complimented. But compliments have been used by speakers so often that they've become stale. Worse, many such openings are clearly so artificial that many listeners don't listen to them today.

To be effective, a compliment must be sincere. To make it so, it should contain honest praise for specific and worthy features. If you are going to compliment your audience, mention a common goal, a recent honor, or perhaps a successful campaign they've achieved. If you're complimenting their town, the very least you can say—clearly and correctly—is the name of the town! Better, mention some feature—the new mall, the recent winning of the "most livable" title, or such. Every hamlet has some distinctive, attractive feature. Mention one or a few, if you are to present a compliment with real effectiveness. You might even compliment the hall in which you speak, if it has some historic significance or distinctive design, for example.

The point is to avoid using old, trite openers which so many speakers have given for so many years—openings which usually come in words such as these:

Well just let me start by telling all of you how really happy I am to be here in your fine town, speaking to you in this really fine auditorium, speaking to just about the finest audience I've ever had the pleasure to address!

"Sleep time!" is the signal received by many in that audience. They've heard such openings so many times. Often they come from speakers who are not quite sure which town they're in; not sure of the differences between an auditorium, a theater, and a hall; not sure just who is out there listening to them.

What makes such openings so bad is their lack of specifics. It's an opening which can be delivered with equal vigor to a group of ecologists or a conference of oil-well drillers. It can be said in San Francisco or Saskatchewan. It will fit the beautiful, gigantic Chandler Pavilion in Los Angeles or a grange hall in Idaho.

9. Using a gimmick

Novelty openings—usually presented with the help of a visual or audio aid—can be especially effective attention-getters. They work on more than just the ears of your listeners. They appeal, also, to their eyes, sometimes even to their noses.

Examples from speeches I've heard over the years include:

Tearing a $100 bill in half as an attention-getter to a speech on banking.

Starting a controlled fire to introduce a talk on safety.

Releasing a pigeon to fly around the room to introduce a presentation on how to train animals.

What makes such openings effective is their shock value. They are unexpected, usually, because they're used so rarely. A creative gimmick can indeed help make your speech memorable. But there are hazards.

A speaker talking to a group in a small classroom opened a talk about refereeing by firing off a blank in a pistol; his point was the importance of knowing the rules. But the loud sound reverberating around the small room hurt the ears of several of his listeners. Others were frightened. Few could concentrate on his words for several minutes. After his speech, there was more talk about his attention-getter than his ideas.

Still, such gimmick openings do indeed get the attention of an audience. Just be sure you use ones which are safe. And legal. And workable. Try them out at home, on your family or friends before you attempt something spectacular before an audience.

10. *Emphasizing the importance of the subject*

This opening is last on the list because it's been overused so much. Furthermore, simply telling an audience that what you have to say is important rarely impresses them. Indeed, if you have to tell them your speech is important, it may well be that it really isn't very important!

Typical of this opening are such lines as:

My topic today is of tremendous importance to every individual here in this hall—and to Americans across the nation, as well.

In the next few minutes I'm going to talk to you about the most important decision you'll ever make.

Yes, they do arouse a bit of interest. After reading those, you may be wondering, *What comes next? What's the speech about?*

But unless your topic does indeed live up to those introductions, you may have difficulty getting your audience to believe—to accept—much of what follows.

As frequently used as this technique is, you'll usually find it better not to tell your audience your subject is important, but to show them, through startling statistics, unusual facts, a moving story, or one of the other techniques for presenting an attention-getter.

Now that you've got the attention of your listeners, it's time for you to introduce the subject of your speech. To get there—to move from your attention-getter to your topic—you need a *transition*.

A transition is usually but a brief sentence or two which connects your opening to your statement of the subject of your speech. Typical transitions include:

That story shows how important it is that we now consider the new guidelines for our budget that I'm going to present to you this evening.

Those figures all point to one clear and necessary reform . . .

You, too, may have come to realize that . . .

The point is clear . . .

Your transition should be followed, in an effective speech, by a clear, specific, precise statement of your speech subject. In the outline speech format which we've been building, it's the second point in the introduction part of your speech:

```
FORMAT FOR A SPEECH
    I. Introduction
       A. Attention-getter
       B. Preview
```

The *preview* of your speech should usually be but a sentence or two long. You can use either of two techniques. First, you can state the point of your speech, your purpose in speaking, the central idea, your viewpoint, or the subject. For example:

This evening I want to talk with you about how we can increase activities by our organization.

My purpose in speaking before you today is to gather support for the new park which is proposed for our town.

My basic point is this: We must vote against the plan to annex more land.

How can you get active in this hobby? Let me brief you.

My subject this evening is noise pollution and how we can stop it.

Many speakers begin their speeches with such openings, using them as attention-getters. That's effective *if* you're sure your audience is already interested in your subject. But a direct statement of your topic—without an interesting attention-getter—may turn off many of your listeners. Some may think, *Increase activities— that's not my problem!* Each of those other topics may just as easily be rejected—mentally—by some in your audience.

Furthermore, starting with your speech topic rather than an attention-getter leaves it up to your listeners to decide if they want to listen. The point of the attention-getter, remember, is to try to guide them to wanting to hear what you've got to say.

The second technique you can use to preview your speech is to list—briefly!—the main points of your speech. Here are some examples:

There are three points to consider about this proposal—who will administer it, who will pay for it, and how it will be evaluated.

Let's consider for a few minutes just what is meant by no-fault insurance—how it works and how it helps you.

Let me tell you why it is a myth that sailing is expensive; why it is a myth that sailing is difficult; why it is a myth that sailing is dangerous.

Blunders

In those two parts of the introduction of your speech —in the attention-getter and the preview—you can probably make more errors which can do more harm to your speech than in any other part of your speech. To avoid problems, follow these Tips:

1. ***Don't be long-winded.*** The introduction of your speech should be only about fifteen percent of your entire talk. Most of us speak about 150 words-a-minute, so in a twenty-minute speech you have around 450 words in which to get your listeners' attention and to let them know exactly what you're talking about.

2. ***Don't antagonize or offend your listeners.*** Unless you want to hazard a shock treatment to get their attention, don't start out, for example, by telling them that their recent action was wrong, or that they are about to waste a lot money, or other such negative openings. True, some speakers are effective in hitting their audiences hard and fast with words that may shock them into listening. But they also run the risk of shocking some listeners into rejecting ideas no matter how logically presented, no matter how well-documented.

Other statements may be insulting to an audience, such as:

> To tell you the truth, I really didn't have time to prepare for this talk, but let me try to tell you what I think.

You are, in effect, telling those listeners that they weren't important enough for you to prepare for them.

3. ***Don't use irrelevant material.*** This is most frequently done by the speaker who tells a joke that has no connection with his speech subject. Or by the speaker who says something such as:

> In going through material for this speech, I found this unusual fact—it doesn't really relate to what I want to say, but I thought you'd be interested in hearing this.

The point is, of course, that everything you say in your speech should be included only on the basis that it does indeed have a direct bearing on what you're talking about.

4. *Don't do a pointless time check.* It was way back when I was in high school that I observed that the more concerned a speaker is about the time he has to speak, the longer he is likely to run overtime. I've seen a speaker step up to the lectern, make a big show out of taking a watch off his wrist. Then he'll wind it, sometimes even hold it up to his ear as if to make sure it's running. Then he'll turn to whomever introduced him and say something such as, "Let me be sure that I don't keep this fine audience overtime—exactly how long is my speech to be?"

Almost always, that's the speaker who rambles on and on. He'll run into the time assigned to the next speaker. He'll even keep an audience well into lunch time.

To avoid being such a speaker, you should of course time your speech in rehearsal. Tips on how to do that —plus time run-overs which are reasonable—are presented in Step 7—Practicing Your Speech.

5. *Don't show your ego.* Speakers do that through such wordings as:

I'm certainly glad to be speaking to you today because just yesterday, in Washington, I was telling Ronnie how he should . . .

Another variation is the show of ego through a put-down. It goes something like this:

It's sure good to be back here at my old high school to speak to you today. Say, does old Miss . . . still teach here? I remember years ago when I was in her class, and she kept telling me how I'd never be a success, and now, here I am . . .

Many speakers put more time in planning the introductions to their speeches than in any other part. The introduction is that important. Work on it carefully. Starting out with a good introduction can increase significantly the effectiveness of the rest of your speech.

CHECKPOINTS:
BEGIN YOUR SPEECH

To help make sure you begin your speeches effectively, use the following guides.

_____ 1. Start with a good attention-getter.
Use one of these techniques:
  _____ (1) Stating a startling fact.
  _____ (2) Asking a question.
  _____ (3) Telling a joke.
  _____ (4) Presenting a quotation.
  _____ (5) Giving an example, illustration, or story.
  _____ (6) Referring to the occasion.
  _____ (7) Pointing to an historic event.
  _____ (8) Complimenting the audience.
  _____ (9) Using a gimmick.
  _____ (10) Emphasizing the importance of the subject.
_____ 2. Use a transition from your attention-getter to your Preview.
_____ 3. Preview your speech.
_____ 4. Avoid these blunders:
  _____ (1) Don't be long-winded.
  _____ (2) Don't antagonize or offend your listeners.
  _____ (3) Don't use irrelevant material.
  _____ (4) Don't do a pointless time check.
  _____ (5) Don't show your ego.

8

STEP #6: Plan the Ending of Your Speech

> *I have never been hurt by anything I didn't say.*
> CALVIN COOLIDGE

TELEVISION NEWS DIRECTORS, when sending a camera crew to cover a speaker, will often tell them, "We'll want to use just a bit of the speech, so be sure to tape everything said in the conclusion."

If any part of a speech gets on TV, it's most likely to be an excerpt from the conclusion.

You may never give a speech that is newsworthy enough for TV. Still, many listeners focus their attention mostly on the ending of speeches. They start to listen more intently when a speaker says something such as, "And so, in conclusion, let me say . . ."

Thus, the ending of a speech is quite important. It should be worded carefully. It should climax the speech. And it should be brief.

The conclusion of your speech usually should be no more than ten percent of the entire speech. That means that for a twenty-minute speech, the conclusion is generally only about two minutes in length—about 300 words.

But remember, that's not an iron-clad rule. Sometimes it's effective to present a very brief, to-the-point, punch conclusion. In other speaking situations, a conclusion which is, say, fifteen percent or more of the speech might be appropriate. Concluding a complex subject with many main points is one example. Or, a long conclusion may be appropriate when a strong appeal for action by the listeners is needed—a call to contribute money, join an organization, or take part in a demonstration, for instance.

The conclusion of a speech is, you'll remember, the third main part of your speech. In that skeleton outline for a speech we've been following, it is the material which is underlined here:

FORMAT FOR A SPEECH

    I. Introduction
       A. Attention-getter
       B. Preview
   II. Discussion
       A. Main points
       B. Arranged logically
       C. Supported with data
 III. Conclusion
       A. Review
       B. Memorable statement

Here are the techniques you can use to make the *review* of your speeches most effective.

1. State that you are about to conclude.

Say something such as "And so, let me summarize," and almost all your audience will listen more closely. Some will think, *This is the part I should remember.* Others may think, *Gee, I haven't figured out what this guy has said so far, so I'd better concentrate now!*

Other phrases that tell your listeners you're about to end your speech include:

Now, let me restate my three main points . . .

To bring what I've said all together in just a few words, let me say this . . .

And so, what have we learned today? First . . .

Some speakers shy away from pointing out to an audience that they're about to conclude. If they are major personalities, outstandingly interesting speakers, or have some other truly major attraction, their listeners may be disappointed that the speech is about to end. But such speakers are rare. Far too many of us go on speaking far too long. Almost always, pointing up a conclusion helps focus both the speaker's ideas and the audience's attention.

2. *Summarize the main idea of your speech.*

This can be as simple and as brief as:

And so you can now see why I'm against this proposal.

Thus I have built the case for limiting the number of commercials on television.

Now you know a bit more, I'm sure, about the life of this great woman.

Those are the reasons I now urge you to join us in stopping the expansion of that shopping center.

Often, that's all the summary a speech needs. Or, you can combine that restatement of your main idea with this technique:

3. Repeat your main points.

Here you say again—in either the same words, or in different wording—the two to five main points you presented in the discussion part of your speech. You might say, for example:

So remember, please, those three keys to successful learning: commitment, regularity, and keeping track of your progress.

Such is the history of educational television—its decade of infancy, its decade of expansion, and now, its decade of excellence.

Think again of what the evidence has shown—the driver was over-tired, his bus was poorly maintained, and his passengers were distracting him.

4. Combine a summary with a repetition.

Many speakers find this most effective. They'll say, for example:

Those, then, are the three reasons why you should invest in mutual funds. First, they provide safety because they are diversified. Second, they provide participation in the growth of our nation. And third, they'll provide you with more money.

And so, through research in libraries in Europe, then through exploration in the area itself and, finally, through computer analysis of tides, currents, weather, and ship characteristics, we now know positively that Columbus' ship lies here, at this very spot on our chart.

Let me repeat: We must improve our harbor. Its needs are clear. It needs better management, better policing, better maintenance.

After your review, present a *memorable statement*. This is your tag, your last statement. It should be both brief and memorable.

1. *Any of the techniques suggested as attention-getters for the introduction of your speech might be used:*

1. Stating a startling fact
2. Asking a question
3. Telling a joke
4. Presenting a quotation
5. Giving an example, illustration, or story
6. Referring to the occasion
7. Pointing to an historic event
8. Complimenting the audience
9. Using a gimmick
10. Emphasizing the importance of the subject

2. *Consider returning to the theme of your attention-getter.*

If you opened with a joke, you might repeat it with a different punch line. If you opened with a quote, you could now add the next line. If you presented an impressive statistic, you might project that statistic. For example:

Just about a half-hour has passed since I began this talk. You may remember the statistic I gave you as I started this speech—that many educational television stations cost more than $100,000 a month to operate. That's educational television. Now let me point out that a commercial TV network spends more than three times that—some $300,000—just for the commercials presented in just the thirty minutes I've been talking.

Or you might adapt the technique of Paul Harvey, television and radio commentator who presents, among other programs, "The Rest of the Story." You might conclude a speech with a story such as:

Remember that young professional football player I told you about to open my speech—the fellow who had won America's highest athletic awards and, at the same time earned his university's highest academic achievements? You may be interested to know that due to a childhood illness, he was not able to run, walk, or even crawl until he was in junior high school!

3. Point to the future.

President Kennedy and his brother, Robert, both closed many of their speeches by looking to the future through the words of George Bernard Shaw:

Some men see things as they are, and ask, "Why?" I dare to dream of things that never were, and ask— "Why not?"

Pointing to the future is often a good way to lead your audience into a discussion. For example:

Those, then, are the problems that exist in our community today. But now, how can we solve them? What action can we here today take? Who in our audience has the first suggestion?

4. Call for action.

This is especially appropriate for the ending of a speech to persuade—a sales talk, a speech to get your listeners to sign a petition or take some other action. Television commercials often close with a call for action:

So rush out right now to your local drugstore and buy a bottle of this new, effective diet aid.

First thing tomorrow, be sure you go to vote—and that you cast your vote for Ms. Johnson.

Call now to get this record at this special price!

5. Consider tie-ins with whatever may follow your speech.

Be alert to what may follow after you've finished speaking. If you're talking about taxes and the group is to have a business meeting after your speech, you might say something about the relationship of the topics. If you're in a debate, with someone about to speak on the viewpoint opposite to yours, you might say something such as:

In a moment, you'll be hearing the reasons against my proposal. As you listen, keep in mind the four reasons I just gave you for our need for this plan. . . .

BLUNDERS you should leave for some other speakers to commit:

1. Don't change the style of your speaking.

Some speakers suddenly change their delivery when they reach the conclusion of their speeches. They may have been informal, humorous, conversational up to the ending. Then they seem to turn almost into another speaker. They become formal. Serious. That confuses many listeners.

The remedy is clear. Follow that first basic principle of almost all successful professional speakers: Don't try to talk like anyone other than yourself.

2. *Don't tell your listeners that you've forgotten some point.*

Speakers often add, late in their speeches, such lines as:

And one thing more I wanted to say was . . .

Oh, and I forgot to tell you that . . .

I did mention, didn't I, that . . .

Those statements point up that you're not as prepared as you should have been. They detract from the effectiveness of your speech.

If you really must add something, try to work it in so it sounds like a planned part of your speech. You might say, for example, right after your review:

Those, then, were my main points. But there's one more point which needs special emphasis—a point I haven't presented as yet, but have saved so you may consider it more carefully.

Or, if there is to be a discussion after your speech, or a question-and-answer period, work that forgotten point in then. Perhaps someone will ask a question, or make a comment, which relates to your additional point. Even if it relates only slightly, you might say something such as:

You raise a good point, because it relates to another idea which we should consider.

3. *Don't merely stop at the end of your material.*

Instead, finish your speech with a smooth, polished ending. Wrap it up—like a package with a nice bow on top. Just stopping your talk after you've presented the last of your ideas and data is jarring to your listeners. They expect you to restate your ideas and then leave them with something worth remembering.

4. Don't apologize.

Don't be one of those speakers who end with such lines as:

Well, that's about it—except I'm sorry I wasn't able to dig out more facts on this . . .

Anyway, next time we get together, I hope I'll have more time to prepare, so you'll really be convinced that we should . . .

Even if you were insufficiently prepared, even if you did need more data, don't tell your listeners. Some may not have noticed your shortcomings—so why put yourself down?

5. Don't stretch it out.

The speaker who doesn't know when to sit down is one of the worst of all speakers, in my opinion. He rambles. He wanders. He adds new points. He restates old points—at length, sometimes restating the restatements.

Repeat your points, sure. But briefly. If you can't state each one in, say, around ten words, you may not have them clear enough in your own mind.

End your speech with a short summary.

End your speech with a statement your listeners may remember.

But most of all —end your speech!!!

CHECKPOINTS:
CONCLUDE YOUR SPEECH

Use the following checkpoints to help insure effective conclusions to your speeches.

_____ 1. Review your speech.
Select from these techniques:
     _____ (1) State that you are about to conclude.
     _____ (2) Summarize the main ideas of your speech.
     _____ (3) Repeat your main points.
     _____ (4) Combine a summary with a repetition.
_____ 2. Present a memorable statement.
Select from these techniques:
     _____ (1) Use one of the techniques used as an attention-getter.
     _____ (2) Return to the theme of your attention-getter.
     _____ (3) Point to the future.
     _____ (4) Call for action.
     _____ (5) Tie-in with whatever may follow your speech.
_____ 3. Avoid these blunders:
     _____ (1) Don't change your style of speaking.
     _____ (2) Don't say you've forgotten a point.
     _____ (3) Don't merely stop at the end of your material.
     _____ (4) Don't apologize.
     _____ (5) Don't stretch it out.

9

STEP #7: Practice Your Speech

*Speech finely framed
delighteth the ears.*

DOUAI BIBLE

THAT ANCIENT PROVERB is still right—practice does make perfect.

But practice also makes work. And takes time. So when you come to practicing your speeches, you can save yourself a lot of work and considerable time by knowing how to practice efficiently.

First, you have to decide how you're going to give your speech—your "mode of delivery," speech professors like to call it. You have three options.

The worst choice, most speakers agree, is the *memorized speech*. First you write out your entire speech word-for-word. Then you commit it to memory.

A memorized speech is used when very exact wording is required, but reading from a script is not appropriate. Such speaking situations are rare today. Still, memorized speeches are presented at many speech contests. The oratorical competitions for high-school students, sponsored by the American Legion, feature memorized speeches. Sometimes a memorized speech is used for presenting an award in a very formal situation.

On some occasions a memorized speech is used to welcome very important visitors. That's when the speaker wants to be very careful of what he says. But it doesn't seem right to read off a script, "We are indeed honored to have you here with us today." Such a speaker wants to be sure to say "honored," not "proud," or "pleased" or any of the many other words that might come to mind if the speech were not memorized.

The advantage of the memorized speech is obvious: You can figure out ahead of time the exact wording you want to use to present every point, tell every tale, state every statistic.

But the disadvantages of the memorized speech are great. It's difficult to deliver with sincerity and warmth. It's hard to keep from sounding as if the speech is memorized. And there is that very big chance that you might forget what you want to say. Fumble one word and you destroy much of the reason for memorizing a speech.

Furthermore, it takes a lot of time and work to memorize a speech. The typical thirty-minute speech has some 4,500 words. Memorizing that would be about the same as memorizing the exact wording of every news story on the first three-and-a-half pages of a typical newspaper.

In sum, don't memorize your speeches. At least not unless it's for some special speaking situation in which you are sure memorizing will be the best method for you to use.

But if exact wording is important, you might try a *scripted speech*. That's written out word-for-word, and then delivered by reading it. That's appropriate when you feel you must use very precise, correct wording, such as a report of negotiations of a union contract, the findings of a scientific study, or the establishment of new policies.

However, you should realize that reading a speech makes it very difficult to sound convincing. Most readers of speeches—as you've probably heard yourself— sound . . . well, they sound as if they're reading! They sound cold, stilted, uninterested. Such speeches often lack sincerity, conviction. When reading, it's very hard to maintain good eye contact and relationship with your listeners.

Another weakness of the scripted speech is that it's very difficult to change on-the-spot, to adapt to the speaking situation. Sometimes when you show up to give a speech, there are conditions which you did not envision when you were writing your speech. You may have expected an audience of several hundred and thought you should speak rather formally; when you arrived, there were but a dozen listeners and the setting was quite informal—a gathering around a table, ties off, drinks and food being passed around continually. You'd sound a bit silly trying to read a speech in such a situation.

Still, there are indeed many speakers who feel more comfortable with a full script from which to read. They feel surer that they won't leave out some key point. Or say something inappropriate. Or fumble a word which might produce a double meaning, an off-color implication. Pacific Telephone, one of the largest of the nation's more than 1,500 phone companies, has a fifty-five-page instruction booklet telling its executives how to give manuscript speeches. It says, "The manuscript speech is clearly the best type of speech for most management presentations." That's true, particularly because such high-level presentations are often written by someone other than the speaker. Indeed, many companies now have full-time speech writers on their staffs.

But most of us don't have a speech writer. We have to prepare our own speeches and we want to do so quickly, easily, and end up with a speech that will be easy to give. So most speakers—by far!—give an *extemporaneous speech*. That's delivered by referring to note cards to remember the specific ideas and information you want to present. But you make up the exact way you'll state those points—the wording of your sentences—as you go along.

The advantages are clear. You're not stuck with having to keep your mind busy pulling memorized words out of your mental storage cabinets. You don't have to keep your eyes glued to a script. You can—easily—

sound much more sincere, personable, confident, author-itative. You communicate to your audience—honestly, realistically—that you do indeed want them to hear and to remember what you say.

The disadvantages of the extemporaneous speech? Some beginning speakers may feel less sure of them-selves. They worry about leaving out important points. Or saying something ineffectively. Or being stuck for words.

But such worries are usually just that—worries, not realities. The fact is that virtually every one of us will give a much better speech, sound more personable, more sincere, more relaxed, more of all the good qual-ities we want in our speeches—if we speak extempora-neously. All it takes to be successful is practice. And here's how to do that.

1. Go over your speech three to six times.

And that's all! If you rehearse the typical speech more than about a half-dozen times it then starts to be memorized. At least parts of it get set in your mind. The trouble with that is if—when you're giving the speech—you can't think of that exact word you've memorized, you feel uncomfortable. You may pause inappropriately. Your face may reveal that you're searching for a word. You may fumble the word, or express the idea poorly.

Practice your speech just enough so you'll be able to glance at those note cards of yours and quickly pick up the idea or information you want to present, look back at your audience, and say what you want to say. Your goal in practicing is to go over your speech just often enough so you can deliver it smoothly and fluently. You don't want to practice until you lose enthusiasm for your speech. Your listeners can spot that lack of fire, often, if you over-practice.

There's a hazard in under-practice, too. If you prac-tice fewer than say three times, you may not implant your speech ideas and information strongly enough on your mind for you to recall them quickly and easily when you face your audience.

2. Practice to remember ideas, not words.

The point of your practicing should be so you'll fix in your mind two things. First, you want to be able to re-call—with a look at your notes—the specific ideas, points, concepts, information you want to say. And the second thing you want to remember is the sequence or order of those points and data.

If you try to remember exact wording, even for parts of your speech, you're moving toward memorizing and all the dangers of that technique. Sure, there may be some wordings you want to present exactly word-for-word—slogans, titles, and such. But if you'll use these practice techniques, they'll probably stick in your mind. If they don't, just take a quick look at your notes to recall the exact wording you want for such points.

3. Practice mentally rather than aloud.

Why? Don't ask. There's been very little research on this technique. Speech specialists apparently don't know why it seems better to go over a speech in your head rather than saying it aloud. Still, many speakers with years of experience claim this works best for them.

Let me tell you how I practice my speeches. I lie down. With note cards in hand, I go over the speech mentally. I don't say the words aloud, not even mut-tered.

Occasionally, over the years, I've tried giving a speech aloud in practice. With the exceptions given in the fol-lowing tips, it doesn't help me. I feel silly standing—even sitting—in my office, talking aloud with no one else there to hear me. I feel really dumb to be talking to myself—practicing a speech—in a motel room at a conference I'm to speak at, for example.

Still, I do want to go over my speech. So I just run through it, mentally rather than aloud.

4. Practice from your actual note cards, not a script.

The emphasis here is on using *actual*—the same—cards you plan to use when giving your speech. Many beginning speakers practice speeches from their outlines. Or they'll make up a set of note cards, practice a couple of times, find they want to make changes in the sequence of points or even the content. So they'll mark up their note cards with arrows showing changes, crossing out some material, writing in some new points. Then after they've got the speech pretty well-rehearsed, they'll write up new note cards. They feel those original cards now have too many changes, and they should speak from nice, neat cards. After preparing the new cards, they figure they're ready to give the speech. Wrong!

Practice at least once—better two times or so—from those new note cards. That practice helps you get a mental image of where each idea and bit of information is located on your cards. If you don't practice with the new cards, your mind will tend to remember the old cards and the location of information on them. Indeed, your arrows, cross-outs, and such further help emphasize in your memory the changes you've made.

The best plan: If you make just a few changes on your note cards—or many changes, but you enter them neatly, carefully—it's far better to give your speech from those original cards. If you must make up new ones, be sure to practice from them at least a few times.

5. Push yourself through the entire speech for each practice.

The usual method for practicing a speech followed by many beginners can be hazardous. They'll start going over the speech, then stop when they get to a spot that they feel they're not expressing clearly, smoothly. So they'll stop the practice, think through how to say that difficult part, get it smoothed out—then go back to the beginning of the speech and start the practice over. This time through they find another rough spot. They stop, polish, and again return to the beginning of the speech and start another run-through. As you can see, they'll soon have that opening practiced a half-dozen or more times before they ever reach the conclusion of the speech. The opening gets polished repeatedly. The closing gets just one or a few practices.

You should, instead, push your mind on through those rough spots in your speech. Start at the beginning of your speech and force yourself through the entire speech. Some places, you'll find, are often a jumble of words which don't make too much sense. Push on through the entire speech anyway. Then, after you've gone through the entire speech, think back to the rough spots. Figure out ways of saying each one in a clearer, smoother wording. Then go through the entire speech again. You'll find most of those rough spots are now smooth, well-worded statements. Oh, a few of the first roughs may still be there, and one or a few new roughs may develop. Spots that were smoothly stated in your first practice may become tangled webs of words in later practices. No matter! Just push yourself through the entire speech, start to finish.

After just a few such complete practices you'll find the whole speech starts developing polish and clarity. You'll have a more precise mental image of your entire speech, rather than just bits and pieces of it. And you'll find this start-to-finish style of practicing takes far less time than other systems.

6. Don't over-practice.

The danger is obvious: over-practice and your speech becomes memorized. Then you'll find your mind struggling to remember specific words rather than ideas. Your delivery, many speakers claim, will sound artificial, flat, uninspired.

7. Don't practice gestures unless you're SURE that will help you.

Most speakers find it *is* helpful to practice gesturing, but not helpful to practice gestures.

The difference? When you practice gesturing, you're training yourself to add interest to your speaking by moving your hands, nodding your head, swinging your arms, and such. That's practicing gestures in general.

That's in contrast to rehearsing a specific gesture to be used at a particular point in your speech. Few speakers find this effective. If you try to practice a pounding of your fist, for example, as you say, "We *must* stop this waste!" both the gesture and the words often appear artificial.

To improve your gesturing in general, try these techniques. First, loosen yourself up by gesturing on almost every word you say—during your private practices, of course, certainly not before an audience. A good technique is to use the same method a baseball player uses just before he steps up to bat. He'll pick up two or three or so extra bats—or add a weight to his regular bat—and take several practice swings. Then he'll put down the extra bats, set aside the extra weight, and find his regular bat feels light, easy to swing. You can use the same technique to practice gesturing.

Run through the alphabet several times. On each letter, try a different gesture. When you say the letter "A" for example, point at the sky; say "B" and nod your head; and so on. Or recite a short, easy poem, gesturing on every word. The idea, remember, is to get comfortable in using gestures. The point is not that you should gesture on every word when you give an actual speech; rather, this is a way to get you to loosen up, to feel comfortable in gesturing as you speak.

8. Don't practice in front of a mirror unless you're sure that will help.

Most speakers find that practicing in front of a mirror distracts them. They find it hard to watch themselves in the glass at the same time they're trying to remember what they want to say in their speeches. Oh, a few speakers find this helpful. You may want to try it. But a far more effective way to see yourself in action as a speaker is to:

9. Tape-record one or two practices.

A tape recorder—so you can listen to how you sound —is helpful. But you'll gain much more if you use a video recorder—a TV recorder—so you can see as well as hear yourself.

Videotape recorders are now becoming popular in many homes. They allow you to make, in effect, a television recording of yourself in action. Golfers use video recorders to improve their swings. Dancers use them to study their movements. Speakers, in particular, find that watching a TV-recording of their speech practices is often their most helpful practice.

Perhaps you already own a video recorder. Or you may know someone who might let you tape yourself. A great many schools—elementary through university— now have such recorders. Try telephoning the audio-visual director at your local school and he or she may be able to arrange a recording. Usually there's no charge—students like and need practice in operating the equipment, and the tapes are reusable, so there's no cost for materials.

Just two cautions. Most people, seeing themselves on TV for the first time, are overly concerned about such minor points as a crooked necktie, mussed hair, a slip that shows. You should, instead, concentrate on the total impact of *what* you say and *how* you say it. Play back your recording three or four or more times so you'll be able to make a more careful, detailed study of your strengths and weaknesses.

Furthermore, many people say, "Oh, I'd be too nervous to watch myself on TV!" The fact is, if you can get past this step—if you can go on to watching yourself on the tape—you'll likely be very pleased with what you see. If you look at yourself with just a bit of honesty, you'll almost surely think, *Well, I don't look like a challenge to Jane Pauley or to Dan Rather! But by golly, I really do look pretty good on TV!*

10. View—or listen to—yourself objectively.

Study the tape, looking for ways you can be still more effective. Answer for yourself—honestly, not over-critically—such questions as:

1. Do you look at your audience—the camera—enough?
2. Do you sound alive, interested, concerned?
3. Do you seem stuck for words only occasionally?
4. Do your ideas come smoothly, logically?
5. Is your speech organized in an easy-to-follow pattern?
6. Do you present a variety of information to support your statements?
7. Do you gesture, move, appear confident, relaxed?
8. Would *you* listen to—be interested in—the speech?
9. Are you using the techniques presented in this book?
10. What can you do to make yourself an even better speaker?

11. Practice using your audiovisual aids.

In the early days of television, when everything went on the air live, before there was filming or video recording, almost every night some announcer would be demonstrating how to operate a lawn mower, for example, and it wouldn't start. Or a can wouldn't open. Or a chart would be shown upside-down.

You, as a speaker, will be like those original TV people—before your audience *live,* without the opportunity to do it over again if your aids don't work.

So practice with your photos, models, charts, whatever. Be sure you know how to work the projector, for example, perfectly. Learn what every knob does on the equipment you're demonstrating. Every once in a while a speaker will show some new gadget, explain how each of the controls on the front of it works. Then someone in the audience will say, "How about that lever on the side—what does it do?" And the speaker is stuck. He didn't practice with all the controls. He fumbles. He's hesitant. His speech has lost much of its impact.

In fact, if the visual is especially important, you might consider having two—one as a backup in case the first one doesn't work. That's especially important in a sales talk, for example. But still, you're going to lose a lot of credibility if you have to turn to that second machine. Best solution: *Be sure* you know how to work everything on your unit, and be sure everything on it works!

12. *Time your speech.*

Most of us speak faster before a real audience than we do during practices. And we tend to state an idea in fewer words when an audience is present. But some speakers do just the opposite—speak slower, use more words, when before an audience.

Furthermore, most speakers find it quite hard to judge the length of time they are speaking. After a speech, some think, *Wow!—I just got up here a few moments ago, and now I'm finished already??!!* But others feel their time before an audience is an eternity.

Usually, you're given at least a general idea of how long your speech should be. The Rotary chairman at a luncheon meeting might say, "You'll have a half-hour.

And please be sure to finish on time because our members have to get back to their jobs." Or the president of the local chapter of the League of Women Voters may tell you, "Be sure to speak no more than twenty minutes—that's all we allowed the fellow who spoke on the opposite view at our last meeting."

So time your speeches as you rehearse them. Most of us speak at about 150 words-per-minute. Thus a five-minute speech has about 750 words—about the same number of words as the typical newspaper feature column. A twenty-minute speech has about 3,000 words —about the length of the average major article in a magazine such as *Good Housekeeping* or *Sports Illustrated*. Those comparisons can help you figure out how much material you can present in your speeches.

You should be able to get the timing of a brief speech exact enough so you'll finish within about ten percent of your assigned time. That means that a five-minute speech should be within about thirty seconds of the intended length. A longer speech, say a twenty-minute talk, should be timed to be within five percent of its assigned length—that is, within one minute of its planned timing.

But a warning: Certainly don't change your rate of speaking just so your speeches will fit into a given time period. If you try to speed up from your usual speed of speaking, you'll likely fumble more words. If you slow down, try to stretch a speech to fill more time, you'll usually lose some of your enthusiasm and smoothness of delivery. Just speak at your own, natural rate.

More than 300 years ago an anonymous Britisher wrote a poem which included the line: "Practice drives me mad!"

Some speakers claim that, too. But no practice is dangerous. Without practice most speakers are not as confident. They worry more about their speeches. Practice builds confidence. And practice helps you get your ideas set in your mind, your words flowing more smoothly.

You can, of course, practice too much. But more speeches suffer from too little practice than too much.

How do you tell how much practice is just right for you? When you feel you're comfortably ready to give your speech, you've probably practiced enough.

It's time to present your speech!

CHECKPOINTS:
PRACTICE YOUR SPEECH

*To help you practice effectively and efficiently,
check the following tips.*

_____ 1. Go over your speech three to six times.
_____ 2. Practice to remember ideas, not words.
_____ 3. Practice mentally, rather than aloud.
_____ 4. Practice from your actual note cards, not
a script or such.
_____ 5. Push yourself through the entire speech
for each practice.
_____ 6. Don't over-practice.
_____ 7. Don't practice gestures unless you're SURE
that will help you.
_____ 8. Don't practice in front of a mirror unless
you're SURE that will help you.
_____ 9. Tape-record one or two practices.
_____ (1) Use an audio recorder, but:
_____ (2) A video recorder will be most
helpful.
_____ 10. View—or listen to—yourself objectively.
_____ 11. Practice using your audiovisual aids.
_____ 12. Time your speech.
_____ 13. Don't change your rate of delivery to meet
a time assignment.

10

STEP #8: Present Your Speech

> *It is but a poor eloquence which only shows that the orator can talk.*
>
> JOSHUA REYNOLDS

SO THE BIG EVENT is here!

You're about to give that speech!!

The chairman is—at this very moment—introducing you. She's telling the audience what a fine speaker you are. How you're a real expert on this subject. How lucky the audience is to have you as the speaker.

But if you're like a great many speakers, you're not hearing much of your introduction. Your mind is rushing from point-to-point in your own speech. You're taking quick looks at your notes—but you don't really see them. Your heart is going faster. Your clothes are fitting tighter. Your mouth is dry. You may decide to take a sip from that glass of water on the table in front of you. But before you can make a move, you hear applause—you've been introduced!

You're on!

There's no stalling time left. This is it!

So—what the heck! Get up there and do your best! And relax. Even have some fun as you speak!!

1. Be yourself.

As you get up to speak, don't try to take on a role different from the real you.

Use your own natural speaking voice. Don't try to pitch it lower, trying to sound like an NBC anchorperson. Don't try to project the authority of a board chairman if you're speaking as a representative of the local PTA.

Don't follow the style of the person who introduced you, or of someone who gave a speech just before you. Some beginning speakers, getting up to talk just after a speaker who was fast-talking, hard-hitting, tend to try to carry on that same style of speech. Don't. Just be yourself.

2. Step up to speak with confidence.

Have you ever seen a television or movie star in person? Almost always, somehow, you can pick them out of a crowd. Most of them seem to project a magnetism or assurance that tends to make us look at them. How do they do that?

Some people seem to be born with those qualities. But most people who project assurance have developed it through practice and experience. It sounds so simple to say, "Think positive and you'll be more positive!" But that does indeed work.

As a speaker, if you'll mentally concentrate—as you step up to speak—on being confident, on being calm, on being assured, you will increase your confidence. But if you worry about stumbling as you get out of your chair, you increase the chances that you will indeed stumble. If you worry about dropping your notes, you tend to increase the likelihood that you will in fact drop those notes.

Some speakers tell themselves, *OK—I'm confident. I'm thinking that. I don't really believe it, but I'm thinking that!* But that bit of mental doubt about yourself can cancel much of the effectiveness of your positive thinking.

Simply *be* assured! Think positive!! You're as prepared as you're going to be for this speech. There's nothing more you can now do to get ready. You've got your ideas as set as they'll ever be for this speech—there's no time for additional thinking. You've practiced as best and as much as you could.

So just get up there and do your very best!

3. Get set before you start to speak.

Most of us feel we have to rush right on and start saying something to those listeners.

Not true.

The audience needs time to take a look at you. Size you up. Get set in their seats. Move their chairs so they get a better view of you. They want—need—a bit of time.

You, too, should take a few seconds to get set. Place your notes on the speaker's stand. Do that slowly, methodically; don't let them get jammed in your pocket, or spill out of order. Take your time.

Look at the mike. If you're short, somehow it always seems that the person who just spoke was tall. Take time to lower the mike. If you can't do it easily—if it remains too high—turn to the chairman and ask her to adjust it for you. For more tips on using that mike, see Chapter Eighteen.

4. Establish contact with your listeners.

Contact is a bond or relationship between a speaker and his or her listeners. Contact comes mostly through looking at individual members of an audience.

Contact, to be effective, should be more than just peering out at all those faces. And it's more than just staring at your audience. It's hard to describe, but both an audience and the speaker know when it's there.

Basically, contact is a mental attitude as much as eyeing your audience. If you look at your listeners with a concern, a feeling, an interest in their hearing and believing what you're saying, contact is much more effective.

Consider your audience as individuals. Let your eyes come to rest for a moment on the eyes of *individuals* in the audience. Look for friendly faces. Spot those who are nodding their heads in agreement with what you say. Seek, too, those who may look doubtful, distrustful, even angry. Eye contact can help you get your ideas accepted.

Contact is something like the relationship you can establish when walking along a crowded street. Look no one in the eye and you continue as just another moving bit of the crowd. Make your eyes meet some of those people you're passing and you'll see a brief flicker of feeling in their eyes. Some may smile. Others will look away immediately. Still, you become more a part of the group, rather than merely one who is moving through it.

Speaking is like that. Your eyes can establish a contact with your listeners that can move you from being just a voice up there delivering audio. Good contact can join you and your listeners together, to become an interrelationship. Then they'll be more receptive to your ideas and information.

5. Begin without referring to your notes.

You've probably been a member of at least one audience when the speaker had to look at his notes to remember to say, "Good evening, it is a pleasure to be here."

You should, instead, step up to the rostrum, get your notes set in place, take a good, long pause to look at your audience with a friendly, assured look, and then begin to speak—without checking your notes for your first words.

Some speakers memorize their opening sentences.

Some, however, still feel they have to look at their notes before speaking. That gives them, as one speaker told me, "Mental assurance that I've got something to say!"

If you feel you just *have* to check your notes before talking, do so—and then take another healthy pause before you speak. The negative-thinking speaker will feel, *But that pause will make me look like I'm trying to think of what to say!* But the positive-thinking speaker can take that pause, collect his thoughts, and project to his audience, *I'm ready to speak just as soon as you listeners look at me as if you're ready to hear me!*

6. Talk WITH, not at, your listeners.

Don't sound as if you've memorized your speech. And don't sound as if you are reading it from a script. Sound extemporaneous—as if you've got your ideas well in mind, and you're now selecting the specific words and phrases to communicate your ideas.

The difference: You should sound enthusiastic, sincere, as if you are speaking spontaneously—sparked by the ideas on your note cards. Your words should be coming from your mind and heart as you speak. Here, in print, it's difficult to express that technique. But you have no doubt heard speakers who sound dull, lifeless, as if delivering a canned, memorized speech. They seldom move their listeners. They rarely get them to believe, to act, to be concerned.

Again, we are considering here a technique that is as much a mental attitude as it is a specific process. Radio and television announcers take special pride in developing the skill of moving from their scripted commercials, for example, to ad-libs—without their listeners noticing a change in their style of delivery. The trick many of those professionals use will work for you.

It is: Keep thinking of your listeners as individuals, not as some large, impersonal "audience." Then, talk *with* them, not at them. This slight but significant difference in your mental attitude of how you view and then communicate with your listeners can indeed move your speeches to be more vivid, successful.

7. Refer to your notes only occasionally.

Many speakers look at their notes much more often than they realize. As soon as they get stuck for a word, they look at their notes. When they make a slip of the tongue, they look at their notes. When they move to a new point, they look at their notes.

Of course you should look at your notes when you need to. But it can quickly become a distracting habit to look at your notes far too frequently.

Better: Pause. Remember that your listeners like pauses. They use the time to digest what you've just said. You can take a moment to think of your next words. You do not have to "keep saying something," as so many speakers apparently feel they must.

Pauses also add authority to your delivery. You seem to be selecting carefully what you are to say. In general, speed in speaking seems to suggest the speaker is less sure, less informed.

If, after you've paused, your next idea, your next words, don't come to mind, of course you should then look at your notes. But take a good, careful, deliberate look. *See* the point, the idea, on your card. Many speakers take just very quick, very brief, glances. They never really see what they're looking at. Indeed, many speakers, told after their speeches, "You sure looked at your notes a lot!" reply, "Come on, I don't remember looking more than maybe once or twice!!"

On the other hand, there's no need to go through an entire speech struggling to not look at your notes. Indeed, in some special situations, looking at your notes can add authority to what you say. If, for example, you're giving a complex statistic or an unusual quotation that many of your listeners may doubt, it may help if you read it directly from your notes. To add even more authority, you might say something such as, "Let's be sure we get this figure correct—let me read it to you from my notes." That's using our well-established belief that if something is written, it seems to be somehow more factual than if we just hear it.

So look at your notes when it's appropriate. Just don't get in that common habit of looking at them all —or most—of the time.

8. Avoid grunts.

"Ah, . . ."
"So."
"Well, . . ."
And the super overused, "Ya know, . . ."

Sure, it is difficult, if not impossible, to get rid of all your little interjections. Just about every speaker puts in some grunts sometimes. But grunts should certainly not be used so often that your listeners start to hear them. They interrupt communication. They distract. They show that the speaker is inept.

If you'll give a bit of thought to why we use them, you'll be better able to control them.

Most of us use grunts to fill in the silence when we take a moment to think of the next word or idea. Grunts give us time, we feel, to get our mind to do its job of selecting the next communication. And that's about all that grunts are—fillers.

Think of the effect if you don't use grunts. You'd pause, saying nothing, as you mentally seek the next words. Many speakers feel those pauses will lead audiences to think they're stuck, that they can't think of what to say. But think of those speakers who do pause like that —speakers who do not grunt, but simply give us a brief silence as they think of their next words. Think of William Buckley. Eric Sevareid. Milton Friedman. Bill Moyers. Their pauses tell their audiences that they're intelligently thinking over what they are about to say. Their pauses suggest authority and assurance.

The solution: *Stop* at the end of an idea. Stop at the end of a sentence. If you need time to think up the next words, pause.

In sum, mind the advice of Oliver Wendell Holmes, American author of the 1800s:

And while you stick on conversation's burrs,
Don't strew your pathway with those dreadful *urs*.

9. *Maintain an appropriate posture.*

If the speaking situation is formal, don't lean on the lectern. Don't cross your legs. Do stand erect. Maintain a professional, authoritative bearing.

If the speaking situation is informal, adapt a casual stance. You might lean on a stool or a table. Crossed arms, crossed legs shouldn't detract. If there are but a few people there to hear you—say a score or so—you might just sit down in a chair, be among your listeners.

The best way to check your own posture is to see yourself on videotape. *"My* posture is *that* sloppy?" more than one speaker has asked himself as he watched a television playback of his speech.

The point: Your posture—like your words, your ideas, your entire speech—should be appropriate to the speaking situation. Ask yourself: Is your posture helping, or is it hindering, your message?

10. *Gesture.*

In the last chapter, you read some tips on how to practice gestures. Here, we remind you to gesture before an audience using those same body movements you usually do automatically when speaking with just one or a few people.

But because of the pressure most of us feel when we speak before an audience of some size, many of us drop all or most of our usual gestures.

That's self-defeating. Gestures will help make you more at ease, as well as improve your communication with your listeners. Note how many people say in conversations, "I *see* what you mean." They may be listeners who can receive a lot of what you say through your movements.

Shakespeare had Hamlet tell a group of actors: "Suit the action to the word, the word to the action." Today, some 400 years later, that's still good advice.

11. Don't fidget.

That includes not only the distracting shifting from foot to foot. Or crossing your arms and then immediately uncrossing them. Or brushing your hand against your hair frequently, or other such bothersome habits. In addition, many speakers will continually shuffle their notes. Or tug at their clothes. Scratch an ear. Run their hand up and down the mike stand. The variety of fidgets can be as diverse as the number of speakers.

Occasionally, fidgeting can add to concentrating the attention of your listeners. Johnny Carson plays with a pencil. But he's turned that fidgeting into a regular comedy bit. He'll flip a pencil in the air, make a wild stab at catching it. He has a dozen or more different routines with his pencils. He's turned his nervous compulsion to play with a pencil into a continuing series of gags.

So fidgeting is a plus for some speakers. But for most of us, fidgeting creates distractions for our listeners.

12. Appear to enjoy speaking.

Audiences can tell—quickly!—if a speaker enjoys speaking with them. They can tell if you really care about presenting your ideas and are sincerely concerned about them as listeners.

Watch those fill-in singers and comedians on television talk shows. Many seem to be simply going through their songs, rushing through their routines. Somehow, you can just tell that many don't really seem to care about what they're singing or saying. And they project an impression that they don't really care if we watch or not. Many of them will stay fill-in performers for a short time, then become carhops or stock clerks.

How do you develop the ability to appear to enjoy speaking? Unfortunately, once again—like so many factors in effective speaking—it depends on your own mental image. Somehow, by *thinking—sincerely*—that you're enjoying yourself, you tend to communicate that feeling to your listeners. It requires you to concentrate on what you're saying. You must feel pleased with yourself. You need to be comfortable with your listeners.

Enjoy yourself as you speak. Be happy to be talking to these particular people. Your enjoyment will come through to your listeners, and your speech will be more effective.

13. *Hide, don't emphasize, your errors.*

Chances are you will fumble a word, or two, or more. We all do it. Listen to the top professional speakers, the anchorpersons on network television. They, too, fumble. Surprisingly often, you'll discover, if you listen carefully. But they're skilled in hiding or minimizing their errors.

Notice what beginning speakers usually do when they make a slip of the tongue. They frown. They sound mad at themselves. They'll make a big point of repeating the word—correctly this time, they hope. But usually they correct with a snarl in the voice, disappointment in their eyes.

Professionals do just the opposite. If it's a minor fumble, they ignore it. If it is important enough to correct, they'll repeat it with a smile, sometimes almost a laugh. They pass it off as unimportant. Which it is. And they'll go right on speaking, not letting the goof bother them.

But the professional will also slow down a bit. He, or she, knows that chances are high that when a speaker fumbles one word, he'll likely fumble another a few sentences later. The beginner speeds up, rushes on, tries to get a lot of words in after the fumble, thinking he's getting the audience to think about something else. But in rushing on, more errors often pile up.

So use the tricks of the professionals. When you fumble, don't let it bother you. Correct the fumble if needed. Don't be mad at yourself. Smile through it. And slow your speaking just a bit. Don't rush on into more fumbles. Get your tongue working smoothly again, your words and ideas flowing. Concentrate on what you're saying, not on how you're saying it. In a word: relax!

14. *Use your aids effectively.*

Be sure all your listeners can see them. Hold them up high. And steady. Many speakers, trying to show a chart to listeners sitting on the far sides of a room, will point the visual at one side for a moment, then before those people have had time to focus in on it and read it, the chart will be pointed to the other side of the room.

Use a pointer to direct your listeners' attention to particular points in your visuals. A pointer adds drama, impact. When you use a pointer, you appear more polished, professional. Besides, pointing with a finger usually puts your arm, often most of your body, between your visual and many of your listeners.

Finally, a simple but important point ignored by many speakers. Talk to your audience, not to your aids. Many speakers, in referring to a diagram, for example, end up speaking to it. Sure, it's acceptable to turn your back on your listeners occasionally. You may have to find a particular spot on your visual. But once you've found it, turn back to the audience to state your point. If you're using a chalkboard, certainly you have to turn your back on your listeners to write on the board. But after you've written a word or two, reestablish visual contact with your listeners.

15. Speak loudly enough.

Your listeners should not have to strain to hear you. For a beginning speaker, how loud is "loud enough" may be difficult to judge. Ideally, get to the room in which you're going to speak well before any of your listeners arrive. Take a friend, put him or her in the back of the room, and try a bit of your speech.

You might even want to have someone signal you as you speak—they could cup an ear, for example, if you get too quiet. But that adds another problem for you to be concerned about during the actual speech, and most of us find that too distracting to be of much real help.

If in doubt, speak a bit louder than you think necessary. Few audiences get unhappy with a speaker who is a bit too loud. But many get mighty restless listening to a speaker they can hardly—or can't—hear. So watch your audience. If they grow restless, speaking up a bit may help.

16. When finished, move out with confidence.

Now that you've just concluded your speech, it's too late for regrets. Don't leave the lectern, return to your seat, with your head shaking in disappointment, your shoulders slumped in regret. Don't start thinking, *Oh, I should have said . . . And I wanted to include . . .*

When your speech is over, maintain your confidence. Walk off like a winner! Hold your head high. Smile. Project confidence. Again, it's a mental attitude. But it can add to, or detract from, the effectiveness of your speech. It's up to you.

Most of us, after a speech, feel we "could have done better." Speakers can find a million faults with their own presentations. That does no good. Not a bit.

The fact is, of course, that we all could have given a better speech—if we had more time, more practice, more help. Once the speech is over, it's over. Take pride in what you've done. You've probably presented as effective a speech as you could, given the time, your resources, your skills. Keep projecting confidence. And if the speech really should have been better, just tell yourself, "The next one *will* be better!" And chances are, it will!

CHECKPOINTS:
PRESENT YOUR SPEECH

A few days before you are to speak, go through the following list, checking off each point to help improve your presentation.

_____ 1. Be yourself.
_____ 2. Step up to speak with confidence.
_____ 3. Get set before you start to speak.
_____ 4. Establish contact with your listeners.
_____ 5. Begin without referring to your notes.
_____ 6. Talk WITH, not at, your listeners.
_____ 7. Refer to your notes only occasionally.
_____ 8. Avoid grunts.
_____ 9. Maintain an appropriate posture.
_____ 10. Gesture.
_____ 11. Don't fidget.
_____ 12. Appear to enjoy speaking.
_____ 13. Hide your errors.
_____ 14. Use your aids effectively.
_____ 15. Speak loudly enough.
_____ 16. When finished, move out with confidence.

11

Speaking Impromptu

> *It usually takes me more than three weeks to prepare a good impromptu speech.*
>
> MARK TWAIN

YOU'RE ON YOUR WAY to a meeting. You're to hear several speakers present their ideas on a subject about which you've got a lot of information. You're relaxed. They're on the spot. They have to speak. All you have to do is listen. And not very hard, at that—you'll probably know much of what they'll say. Still, you figure it will be fun to listen to them.

You walk into the meeting a few minutes before it starts. Big audience—must be a lot of interest in the subject.

The chairman—an old friend of yours—rushes up to you. "Our main speaker just called—he missed his plane! He can't get here to give his speech! I'm really in a spot. Please—will you fill in?"

An impromptu speech!

What do you do? How can you prepare in just a few minutes? How can you say something worthwhile on such short notice?

Well, it's not as difficult as you may think.

Realize, first, that you're not likely to be asked to speak on the spur-of-the-moment—to give an impromptu speech—unless you know something about the subject. Sure, when you were back in high school or college you might have had a class or two in which you'd be asked to suddenly stand up and speak on a topic you really didn't know much about. But in the real world that rarely, if ever, happens.

Realistically, you might be asked to speak impromptu in a situation such as this. You were chairman of last year's fund raiser, and now you're at a meeting to plan next year's drive. You're not on the committee this time, so you don't expect to speak. But with your experience, you just might be asked to give your ideas on how to improve the event, for example.

Another typical situation in which you might give an impromptu speech is when you're listening to speakers who you feel are leaving out one or more critical points. You feel you just can't sit there and let them go on ignoring some significant point. You're moved to stand up and speak—to give an impromptu speech.

Those examples point to *the basic tip* for giving impromptu speeches:

BE PREPARED!

Use that old, reliable Boy Scout motto by *predicting* when you might be called on for an impromptu speech. If you received an award last night, chances are that whenever you go to meetings in the next week or so, you might well be asked to "say a few words."

Now this is not to suggest that every time you go some place you should take along a written outline or note cards for a speech you might give. You don't have to be prepared with a full oration to fill in for every little old speaking situation you attend.

On the other hand, if you are informed or experienced on the subject of the meeting, and if there's a possibility that you might be called upon to speak, you just might get yourself ready—at least partially ready.

How?

Some people seem to have mental computers that store

away jokes, gags, quips, strange statistics, unusual experiences, and such. If you're that type, you'll of course use one or a few of them in your impromptu speeches.

If you don't have a mental storehouse, you might find just a couple of appropriate bits of material that you could work into an impromptu speech, just in case you're called on to speak. The best way to build your storehouse is to keep up-to-date in your field. Read regularly at least one of the major magazines in your field of interest and employment. Read at least one newspaper a day, one weekly news magazine a week. Watch TV network news and your local news program, too. Know what your company is doing; read its newsletters, memos, and other communications.

Another technique for being prepared for impromptu speeches: keep a few files of clippings. As you see articles in the papers and magazines which relate to your interests, tear them out, drop them in the files. That will help implant the stories in your mind. And of course you'll have a ready source to look over when you might have to give a speech—impromptu or prepared. Once a year, throw away out-of-date clippings. Or, start a new file each year. This doesn't have to be a big project. You don't have to include everything that appears in print about your fields of interest. These files are merely backups, not all-inclusive research.

Realize, also, that virtually always your listeners know that the speech you're giving is impromptu. That's revealed by the situation—by what the chairman says when he calls on you or introduces you, by your volunteering to speak, or such. So your audience will be sympathetic. They're not expecting a full-blown oration.

Still, giving a good impromptu speech can do much to add to your image. Sound smooth and polished in an impromptu speech and people are impressed. Use the following platform-tested techniques and you should make a pretty good impromptu speech.

1. Take a few moments to get your ideas focused.

As soon as you agree or decide to give an impromptu speech, you should try to get off someplace by yourself to think through what you're going to say. Best: Go for a walk, find a lonely corner in the hall, or seek some other spot where you can think without distractions.

If the meeting's already started and you're sitting there in the audience, for example, you probably can't walk out—you'll miss what other speakers say, and you may appear to be leaving. But you can turn off most of your mind—listen with one ear, use the rest of your brain to organize your ideas.

Occasionally you may be called upon to speak with no notice ahead of time at all. Still take at least a few moments to collect your thoughts. A chairman might say, for example (a rude, unthinking chairman, indeed —but it happens!)—"I see Bill sitting out there in the audience, and I know he's concerned about this problem. Bill, we hadn't planned on your speaking this evening, but I just thought you should be asked to stand up and give us your ideas."

Well, stand up—but you don't have to start speaking immediately. Take time to mentally select what you are to say. The audience will wait; many will be impressed by your thoughtfulness.

2. Decide what the main point of your speech will be.

If you are to present a viewpoint on a controversial topic, decide—quickly—if you're going to be for it, against it, or noncommittal. If you are to present information, focus on one specific aspect—how the plan works, what you learned from your experiences, what the organization needs. Be as specific, to-the-point as you can.

If you can do it, it's wise to write out the point of your speech. You probably won't have time to work up a full outline. But writing down the point of your impromptu speech will help you focus your thoughts. Writing just one or a few words will help you stay on the topic as you talk. You're more likely to present material which is relevant.

Of course, it's not always possible or appropriate for you to write down even the briefest statement. That's OK. Then just concentrate on saying only ideas and information which relate to your topic. If a point or a fact comes to mind that you're not sure is relevant, it's often best to reject it—not include it in your speech.

3. *Use the structure of your typical prepared speeches.*

You'll remember that back in Step #4 of how to build a successful speech, this book gave you several basic structures—time, topic, and others.

For an impromptu speech, your speech structure doesn't have to be very formal. Still, one structure stands out as easy to remember and simple to use. It's the:

```
BRIEF KEY TO IMPROMPTU SPEECH
            Past
          Future
          Present
```

That's a time pattern, of course. No matter what the subject of your impromptu speech, those three words—*Past, Present, Future*—can help you organize your thoughts. Here's how.

Speak first—after you've stated your specific viewpoint—about the past of the subject. How did the problem arise? What has been done to solve it before now? Why hasn't it been solved in the past?

Next, talk about the present situation. Why is the problem important now? What's happening now? What incidents, people, situations, etc. have brought the problem or subject to this group's attention at this particular time?

Finally, consider the future. What action do you recommend be taken? What might happen in the future if it isn't solved now? What future benefits can be expected by solving the problem? What might happen if no action is taken?

That *Past, Present, Future* format is certainly not the only way to organize an impromptu speech. But it is a structure—a *BRIEF KEY*—that's easy to remember and will fit any subject.

4. Support your views with specifics.

This may be the hardest part of an impromptu speech. Still, if you can come up—from your own experiences, your studies, beliefs, attitudes, or such—with at least a few statistics, examples, stories, or other bits of data, you'll add much to your speech. As with all speeches, data add authority and believability.

Try not to say—or imply—"I don't really know why I think that's the best action, but I do." Instead, try to build at least a bit of a case of logic based on specifics. You need not be precise. If you're speaking on one side or the other of changing the fifty-five-mile-an-hour speed limit for cars, for example, you don't have to remember that exactly 52,411 people were killed last year in auto accidents. You might say, "As I remember it, somewhat more than 50,000 people were killed." Or, "I forget the exact figure, but I know I've read that tens of thousands are killed each year in car wrecks."

5. Tie in with the other speeches.

Suppose you're at a public meeting to decide how to use an abandoned railroad track that passes through your town. Some speakers have urged that the rails be ripped up, the area paved, made into a jogger's path. Others have spoken in support of leaving the tracks, running a small, historic train to the next town—to serve locals as they shop, tourists as they sight-see. You're in the audience, listening to both sides. You can tell that they're never going to agree, if they keep on talking as they are. But you think you have a solution which would be acceptable to both sides. You're moved to make an impromptu speech. If you can tie your speech in with the previous speeches, chances are higher that you'll bring about a solution. What can you say?

You can point out that both sides stated they're "interested in getting the most value possible for the most people." Another point of agreement: "We don't want this to cost a lot of tax money." Very often, two sides arguing their own views never hear such points of agreement; they're too intent in trying to be sure their own proposals are established.

So you might bring about a solution by pointing to those two points of agreement, then adding that the rough railroad ties between the rails could be paved over and the rails kept. Joggers could run in the middle, the train could run on the tracks, and with just, say, six trains a day, they'd not interfere with the joggers very much.

Thus, by pointing to statements speakers made in previous speeches, you might be able to give an impromptu speech which brings agreement and a solution.

6. Take your time.

There's no need to rush this speech at all. Take good, long pauses—as you stand up, after your opening statement of your viewpoint, after each of your points and specifics. Take time to think through what and how you're going to say the next sentence or so. Your listeners are interested—by the very nature of the situation —in your ideas. They'll wait for you to get your thoughts in mind.

7. Keep cool.

Accept the invitation with assurance. Frankly, most of the time you can't get out of giving an impromptu speech once you're called upon. Or at least it's awkward or uncomfortable or even impolite to refuse. So, make up your mind to make the best of the situation.

Your audience will think you're every bit as assured as you appear. On the other hand, if you hesitate, if you try to beg off from speaking or stall for time, many listeners may become both impatient and doubtful of at least some of what you say.

Relax. You're not expected to hold that audience spellbound. You're not expected to cram them with a pile of facts. You're not expected to present a perfectly clear, logical, formal address. Just say your say—*AND:*

8. Sit down when you're finished.

Obvious? Sure. A point missed by many speakers? Indeed!

You've heard them—going on and on, saying something such as:

> Well, that's all I really have to say about this. Like I said, I think it's a good idea—we should do it. I'd like to tell you more, but I can't think of anything else. Still, we should certainly do it. There's nothing, really, I can add to that, except to say, again, that . . .

Stop! You said your say, so sit!

BLUNDERS

Avoid these frequent BLUNDERS of impromptu speaking:

1. Rambling

The worst case, probably, is the speaker who's asked for his views about a controversial subject, but he just can't—or won't—take a position. He'll often ramble on with such foolishness as:

So, sure, I guess we should adopt this plan. It is sure better than what we're doing now. Of course we've been holding together pretty good all these years doing the way we have, and so that must be at least fairly good—we could just leave things as they are. And we have to recognize that there sure are some problems—cost, and personnel, and a new plan usually brings more problems—if we do adopt this plan. So maybe we should all think it through and maybe we'll find it really isn't such a good idea.

Come on, fella, take one side or the other! And get to the point! If that's the best you can say, don't say it! Follow the advice of the Greek philosopher Dionysius —some 400 years B.C. He said: "Let thy speech be better than silence, or be silent."

2. Getting off the subject

This is a near cousin to rambling, but different. And to be avoided—definitely!

Getting off the subject is frequently the escape route taken by the speaker who wants to talk, but doesn't have anything to say—that is, he has nothing to say about the subject being considered. So he'll proclaim—usually long and loud—something such as:

This new rule about membership that we're considering is really important. I'm not really sure what we should do about it, but one thing I know—it's something like what happened one time when I was out in the Pacific. Sure, that was a long time ago, and I don't remember all the details, but let me tell you. We were stuck on this tropic island and we needed to send a radio message. There were ten of us, and only two knew how to work the radio. But one of them . . .

Well, maybe there is a relationship between a membership rule and operating a radio, but so far the speaker hasn't stated just what that connection is.

3. Apologizing

Almost always, the speaking situation makes it clear to everyone in the audience that you're giving an impromptu speech. So very rarely is it appropriate for the impromptu speaker to apologize for not being prepared.

It's certainly obvious you're speaking impromptu when you are a member of the audience, and you stand to state your views. And when someone asks you to fill in for a missing speaker, he usually tells the audience that you're filling in on the spur of the moment.

Should you ever run into a chairman who is a real clod—one who tries to pass you off as just another prepared speaker—then you should certainly correct that error early in your speech. You might say, "Oh—one thing our chairman overlooked saying, and I'm sure he'd want you to know, I wasn't scheduled to speak this evening, but one of the speakers didn't show up, and so I was asked—just about ten minutes ago—to fill in." But then don't add an apology. Don't say something such as, "So I'm not really as ready to speak as I could be, but I'll do my best." That merely puts yourself down. It does not enhance your speech.

Your listeners, once they know just the fact that you were given little time to prepare, will make an allowance for your limited preparation. Indeed, some audiences have been won over to a viewpoint simply because an impromptu speaker presented a pretty good case, while the prepared speakers either presented just equal or inferior speeches. Occasionally an over-polished speaker, appearing to the audience as too-prepared, too loaded with facts, may turn an audience to accepting the ideas of a speaker talking impromptu.

4. Acting surprised

Even if the impromptu speech is a real surprise to you, don't act as if it is. Fumbling, wandering explanations don't add anything to your image or your audience's knowledge or viewpoint. Don't say such things as:

> Well! I sure didn't really expect to talk here this evening. This is really a big surprise to me. I hadn't thought that I'd be called on to say a few words. I'm really sorry that . . .

All that verbiage does no good whatever. Besides, you should remain alert to speaking situations in which you might be called upon to speak. Remember: *BE PREPARED!*

Some readers may think, *Come on, this impromptu speaking sounds like a lot of work!* Well, depends upon how you look at it. Around a hundred years ago American humorist Mark Twain said:

> It usually takes me more than three weeks to prepare a good impromptu speech.

CHECKPOINTS:
IMPROMPTU SPEECH

When you're about to go to a meeting at which you might be called upon to give an impromptu speech, take a moment to go through the following points to help insure you'll give a more effective speech.

Before going:

_____ 1. Predict when you might be asked to speak impromptu.

_____ 2. Be prepared!

When called upon:

_____ 1. Take a few moments to get your ideas focused.

_____ 2. Decide what the main points of your speech will be.

_____ 3. Use the structure of your typical prepared speeches.

_____ 4. Remember:

BRIEF KEY TO IMPROMPTU SPEECH
Past
Present
Future

_____ 5. Support your views with specifics.

_____ 6. Tie in with the other speeches.

_____ 7. Take your time.

_____ 8. Keep cool.

_____ 9. Sit down when you're finished!

_____ 10. Avoid these blunders:

    _____ (1) Rambling.

    _____ (2) Getting off the subject.

    _____ (3) Apologizing

    _____ (4) Acting surprised.

12

Introducing a Speaker

> *Wise men talk because they*
> *have something to say; fools,*
> *because they have to say*
> *something.*
>
> PLATO

IF SOMEONE IS keeping a record book of the *worst* speeches of all time, certainly the usual introduction of guest speakers must be at the top of the list. Speeches introducing a speaker are often boring, trite, forgettable. But they don't have to be.

When you introduce a speaker, you can give a good speech. You can arouse interest in the guest speaker. You can present solid content and specific information. You can be clever and use humor with taste.

Here's how.

First, keep in mind the purpose of your speech. It should have a two-way goal. Most people simply introduce the speaker to the audience. It's much better to introduce the audience to the speaker, as well.

That follows the same basic technique used for introductions in one-to-one social or business situations. You don't just introduce one person to the other. Rather, you introduce both people to each other. You say something such as: "Mike, meet Jim Oaks. Jim's been sailing off the coast here for ten years. Jim, this is Mike Atlas. Mike was asking how he could start sailing." Two-way introductions should be the rule when you're introducing a guest speaker and an audience.

Your speeches of introduction should answer these four questions in the discussions part:

1. Why this speaker?
2. Why this subject?
3. Why this audience?
4. Why at this time?

You don't have to present the answers in that order in every introduction of a speaker. If the subject of the guest's talk may seem to be rather far from the interests of the audience, you'll probably find it best to answer first the question, "Why this subject?" Or you may be introducing in June a speaker who is to give tips on shopping for Christmas, so you might make the first point in your introduction the answer to "Why at this time?"

Whatever order you answer those questions, remember they are just the discussion part of your speech. This speech, as all others, still follows the same basic format for a speech. Here, then, is the complete structure:

FORMAT FOR INTRODUCTION SPEECH

I. Introduction
   A. Attention-getter
   B. Preview
II. Discussion
   A. Why this speaker?
   B. Why this subject?
   C. Why this audience?
   D. Why at this time?
III. Conclusion
   A. Review
   B. Memorable statement: formal
      introduction of the speaker

Here's an example of how that structure would be applied. Let's say you're to introduce a visiting college professor. She's an expert on noise pollution. Assume that she's to speak before your local Chamber of Commerce. Here's what you might say to introduce her.

Is noise getting to you?
Are you bothered by the
yelling on TV commercials?
Is your child's hearing
damaged by loud music?
When you stay at a motel,
does the roar of passing trucks
keep you from getting a sound
sleep? Is our town being
drowned in noise?

I. INTRODUCTION
A. ATTENTION-
GETTER

This evening, we are to hear—
if noise will let us!—about the
latest research about noise.
We'll learn how noise affects
us and what we can do to
control noise. Our speaker is
Dr. Betty Post, Professor of
Engineering at our State
University.

B. PREVIEW

Dr. Post has just concluded
three years of research on
noise. Her findings have been
reported in *Time* magazine.
She's been honored by the
American Medical Associa-
tion. Her research has been
used by two federal agencies.

II. DISCUSSION
A. WHY THIS
SPEAKER?

We read—sometimes we hear
—a lot these days about
pollution. Pollution is filling
our air. Pollution dirties our
streams. Pollution contami-
nates our food. Pollution
assaults our eyes. But there's
still another kind of pollution

B. WHY THIS
SUBJECT?

—noise. It's growing faster, yet controlled less, than any other type of pollution, some experts say.

We here in this audience—as members of our Chamber of Commerce—may be hurt more than anyone else by noise pollution. Not only are our ears damaged and our nerves rattled by noise. Our businesses, too, suffer when noise pollution is high. Our customers are uncomfortable in noisy stores. Our tourists come here to relax, but noise can increase their tensions—thereby making them cut short their stay in our town, and thus reducing the dollars they spend in our businesses, as Dr. Post will show us.

C. WHY THIS AUDIENCE?

Summer—the high point of our tourist business—is still three months away. There are some specific things we can do *now* to reduce noise and increase the attractiveness of our town for ourselves and for our visitors.

D. WHY AT THIS TIME?

Here, to give us some specific suggestions, is one of the nation's top experts on noise pollution. Her subject is important to us, as business leaders. This is a good time for us to begin action to reduce noise pollution.

III. CONCLUSION A. REVIEW

Ladies and gentlemen, the
Chairman of Engineering
Research at State University,
Dr. Betty Post.

B. MEMORABLE STATEMENT— THE FORMAL INTRODUCTION

As you use that model for a speech of introduction, remember that "model" does not mean "perfect." Model means, according to Webster, "something proposed as worthy of imitation." You can make that model introduction closer to perfection by adding more of *you*—your words, your ideas, your specifics.

In addition, here are FIVE TIPS that can help you make your introductions more effective.

1. Set the tone of the meeting through your speech of introduction.

Appropriateness is the major criterion. If your guest speaker is to present ideas on low-cost vacations, your introduction should set a light, pleasant mood for your audience. If the speaker is to talk about the death and destruction that will result from the coming biggest-ever earthquake, your introduction should of course be designed to settle the audience into a serious mood.

2. Know your speech thoroughly.

The assumption is that you, as the introducer of the speaker, know that speaker fairly well—at least better than most people in the audience. Even if that's not true, you are serving in the role of the link between the audience and the speaker.

Therefore, you should certainly not read to your listeners your speech of introduction. In fact, it would be most effective if you didn't have to refer to your notes at all. Frequent glances at your notes to check the speaker's hometown, or degrees, or title, or any such details will detract from your authority and from the effectiveness of your speech.

The best procedure: As usual, outline your speech. But don't write it out. Practice it thoroughly. Get all the points firmly set in your mind. But don't practice it so much that the words are memorized. For details, review Step #7—Practicing.

Most important: Have a note card ready in case you do get stuck. But be sufficiently prepared so you really don't need to look at that card. Instead, consider that card but a mental insurance policy—there *if* you need it. By just being available, that card will help give you the mental assurance you need to give your speech smoothly, fluently, with few or no fumbles.

3. Be accurate.

Few problems can get a guest speaker off to a worse start than if he feels obligated, after your introduction, to make a number of corrections. Don't make him have to say, "Thank you, Mr. Chairman, for that introduction. But perhaps the audience should know that I'm from the State University, not the college; I'm professor of physics, not engineering; and my actual topic tonight is . . ."

Solution: Get the details about the speaker from him in writing well ahead of time. Phone or write to him a couple of weeks before the presentation. Then, check key points with him, in person, when you first meet shortly before he is to speak.

4. During the speech, be attentive.

If the audience's attention wanders from the speaker, for any reason, it will usually center first on you. Remember, as the introducer, you are that audience's link with that speaker. If you're not listening—and listening attentively, appreciatively—many in the audience will follow your cue and not listen, either. Those chairmen who make their introductions, then proceed—as the guest speaker is giving his all—to make notes, confer

with others at the main table, check with the head-
waiter, do anything other than concentrate both eyes
and ears on the guest, are simply helping that speaker
be less effective than he could be. Your deportment,
your attention, your actions should all add to, not detract from, the speaker's efforts.

5. After the speech, express a few words of sincere appreciation.

This should be, of course, a public "thank you" to
the speaker. You should express appreciation on behalf
of the audience.

The key word in this guide is "sincere." If, unfortunately, the guest turned out to be a dull, droning
talker, certainly don't conclude the program by saying
to the audience and the speaker something such as:

Thank you for a truly fine speech. I'm sure all of us
were deeply moved, highly impressed by your very
effective presentation.

That speaker usually knows—and certainly that audience knows—if he deserves such high praise. Say
something, but be sincere—and brief. A simple statement will do:

Thank you, Dr. Baker. We appreciate your coming
here to share your ideas with us.

Enough.

There are six BLUNDERS you should avoid in planning and presenting a speech of introduction.

1. Don't make it a speech about yourself.

A middle-aged businessman, for example, is selected
to introduce as guest speaker a former high-school class-

mate. The guest speaker went on to become a leading quarterback for a major professional football team. Far too often the introducer will go off on an ego trip, introducing the speaker in such words as:

> A lot of you know, I think, that Joe and I went to school together. Of course he was a good ball player in those days, too. I remember one day we were playing against each other, on practice teams. He was in the backfield, I was in the line. I could see the play coming. I really got set. I was ready! And I hit him with a tackle which—well, let me tell you, I really hit him! I stopped him cold. I . . .

And the audience is thinking, *Sure, sure, but who cares about your little victory of years ago! Just introduce that speaker!*

In introducing a speaker, you should avoid all but the briefest and quite modest references to your relationship with the speaker. Certainly don't mention any successes you might have had in winning out over the speaker.

2. *Don't give the speaker's speech.*

Often the introducer is selected to make the introduction because he has some special knowledge or interest in the subject of the guest speaker. That leads many introducers to start talking about their own bits of data, stories, examples, points, ideas on the subject. Before long, the introducer may well have given key points or some significant content that the guest speaker was intending to present.

Simply stick to that formula—Why this speaker? Why this subject? Why this audience? Why at this time? Then you're not likely to ruin the guest's own speech by airing his material.

3. Don't build up the speaker's skills as speaker.

If the audience does need to be convinced that the guest is a good speaker—is worth listening to—that should have been done well before the meeting at which the guest is to speak. You could have told them that at the previous meeting, when the speech was announced or scheduled, for example. Or the speaker's skills could have been advertised in the local newspaper, the club's newsletter, or a mailer announcing the event. All those techniques would have been appropriate.

But right now, with the speaker sitting there before the audience, the audience in just a very few moments will figure out for themselves if the speaker is effective or not. It's far too late to start praising the guest as a speaker.

However, there is one exception to this guide. When you introduce a comedian, he should be introduced with glowing words about his skills at getting the audience to laugh.

A perfect example is related in Dick Cavett's autobiography entitled (surprise!) *Cavett*. For years he'd been a very successful writer of comedy for a variety of stars—Jack Paar, Johnny Carson, Jerry Lewis, and others. Then he took to the stage at a club in Greenwich Village to make his first appearance as a comedian. Result of that first performance: absolute failure. Cavett wrote, "I made two bad mistakes. I asked for the wrong kind of introduction, and I failed to be funny."

What was wrong with that introduction? Cavett says, "I didn't want the audience to expect a harsh one-line comic type, so I told the emcee to tell them there was a young man backstage who would like to talk to them." That serious introduction led the audience to expect a serious speech. They did not laugh. After the show, Cavett phoned his longtime pal, Woody Allen. His advice: "You have to insist on an intro that makes two things clear: That you are a comedian, and that the audience is expected to laugh."

4. *Don't use humor without being positive it's appropriate.*

No, this is not a warning against using off-color jokes. Rather, you are being cautioned that a point you may treat lightly may be one which the guest speaker considers very serious.

One time I heard an academic dean introduce a guest speaker at a faculty meeting which was considering a new course of study. Earlier that week the faculty had met to debate the problem of sexist language in the group's constitution. It included lines such as, "If a member wants to introduce an amendment, he shall . . ." A few women in the faculty objected to that wording. They wanted such statements to be written as "(s)he" or "he/she," or "they" (clearly a basic error in grammar), or in some other nonsexist wording. The chairman considered this problem minor. But the guest speaker thought it very serious indeed. In his introduction, the dean tried for a bit of humor by saying, "Our speaker today got her—whoops!—remember our meeting of a few days ago! I guess I should say '*it* got *its* training at . . .'" The guest immediately took strong offense to the remark. She spent nearly a third of her speech lecturing us on her ideas about sexist language. The result: The audience heard very little from the speaker about the main subject for this meeting—remember?—that new course of study.

Certainly a bit of gentle humor should be included in most speeches of introduction. Humor should be in almost all speeches. But as you've probably heard, being funny is a serious business. It is hard to word, difficult to deliver. Often what's funny to some is tragic to others. It's easy to present humor that's in poor taste.

The best advice: Play your speeches of introduction pretty straight—not arrow straight, but with gentle, surefire humor that you are positive is appropriate.

5. Don't save the speaker's name until last— unless surprise is valid.

Actually, your job in introducing a speaker is not to hide the speaker's name, but to make it very familiar. Work the guest's name into your speech several times. The repetition will help the audience and the speaker feel they already know each other a bit more.

Unless you really are introducing a surprise speaker. If, for example, your group is meeting week after week, with a guest speaker at almost every meeting—as is the custom at so many service clubs and civic groups— audiences soon grow blasé about guest speakers. If they are used to hearing a local politician, a touring college professor, the head of a nearby factory, and suddenly you corner a Joyce Brothers, or a Julian Bond, or an Edward Teller—saving the name till the end of your introduction can be effective indeed. You can, of course, build anticipation, suspense, curiosity about such a speaker. But that won't work unless the guest is truly well known or respected by your audience.

6. Don't forget the name of the speaker.

Most of you have stories and experiences that show the importance of this guide! What *was* it that made me forget the name of my wife of thirty-seven years when I fumbled a social introduction last week?

How do you prevent such forgetfulness? You can't prevent it—but you can reduce the chances. Practice. Use the speaker's name when you first meet him or her. Write the name several times. Think the name. But again, most importantly, most effectively: Use the name.

And, keep that safety net close at hand—your note card. Print the guest's name in big, bold letters! Chances are, just the fact that you've got that backup to your memory will help you remember your old friend— what's his name!!

CHECKPOINTS:
INTRODUCING A SPEAKER

Check off each point as you plan your speech of introduction.

_____ 1. Use this guide:

FORMAT FOR INTRODUCING A SPEAKER

_____ I. Introduction
     _____ A. Attention-getter
     _____ B. Preview
_____ II. Discussion
     _____ A. Why this speaker?
     _____ B. Why this subject?
     _____ C. Why this audience?
     _____ D. Why at this time?
_____ III. Conclusion
     _____ A. Review
     _____ B. Memorable statement:
           formal introduction of
           speaker

_____ 2. Change the sequence of those questions answered in the discussion as appropriate.

_____ 3. Follow these tips:
     _____ (1) Set the tone of the meeting by your introduction.
     _____ (2) Know your speech thoroughly.
     _____ (3) Be accurate.
     _____ (4) During the speech, be attentive.
     _____ (5) After the speech, express a few words of sincere appreciation.

_____ 4. Avoid these blunders:
     _____ (1) Don't make it a speech about yourself.

_____ (2) Don't give the speaker's speech.

_____ (3) Don't build up the speaker's skills as a speaker.

_____ (4) Don't use humor without being positive it's appropriate.

_____ (5) Don't save the speaker's name until last—unless surprise is valid.

_____ (6) Don't forget the name of the speaker!

13

Making an Announcement

> *Blessed is the man who,*
> *having nothing to say,*
> *abstains from giving in words*
> *evidence of the fact.*
>
> GEORGE ELIOT

THIS IS THE SPEECH that the inexperienced speaker often gets pushed into giving. A chairman will ask a member, "Say, you've been attending those planning meetings—how about you making an announcement about the fund drive?" That happens often to the helpful but quiet member. To the manager attending an executive meeting. To the assistant going to a conference. To the newcomer to an organization.

Many speakers, especially beginners, try to make a brief announcement into a major presentation. Don't. Keep it simple. Follow this structure:

FORMAT FOR ANNOUNCEMENT SPEECH

   I. Introduction
     A. Attention-getter
     B. Preview
  II. Discussion
     A. Name of event
     B. Date and day
     C. Time
     D. Location
     E. Cost
     F. Special features
     G. Importance
     H. Other details as needed
 III. Conclusion
     A. Review
     B. Memorable statement

Because you usually don't have much time for this speech, present a very brief *attention-getter*. If you can't find a short, relevant story, joke, or such, use one of those teasers you've heard so many times. Ones like these still work fairly well:

Here are the details about that annual picnic we all enjoy so much.

Next month's meeting is really going to be something special.

Many of you have been asking about the up-coming scholarship drive—well, here are the facts about it.

Often, you can find a good opening line by going through the facts you are to present and picking out the most interesting or unusual. If your group has a local high-school coach speak at each meeting and next time you're having the coach of the professional All-Stars, that should be your attention-getter.

If your announcement is pretty routine and doesn't

include a really interesting point, try a bit of humor. You might say:

> There's some good news and some bad news about our next regular meeting. The good news is that we're going to hold it. The bad news is—that's all the good news there is about it.

Or, you can often draw humor out of something that happened at the last meeting:

> For the three people—shall I name them?—who slept through last month's meeting, let me announce the details about our next meeting, so they can start resting up now.

The *preview,* too, should be very brief:

> We'll have a guest speaker next week.

> The next race will be Saturday.

> A new workshop is to be presented.

In the *discussion,* the facts need not be presented in the order suggested in the format. Generally it's best to put an interesting detail first, followed by more routine specifics. The final fact should usually be another interesting bit.

If the event doesn't have a *name,* try thinking one up. Humor, again, may help your audience remember your announcement. Or giving it a name with a bit of a twist such as:

> Our next speaker, timed for your usual after-lunch nap, will be . . .

> For those of you wondering how to get rid of the extra money you'll have from the tax reduction, we'll hold our fund raiser for . . .

Get that *date* right! Sure, *all* the facts should be correct. But more speakers seem to fumble dates during an announcement than any other point. It will help you clarify the date and also further imprint it on the minds of your listeners if you name the day of the week as well as the month and the number of the day.

Be specific on the *time*. Answer all the questions that might come up—"Will the speaker start at nine or do we have a business meeting first? If I get here a half-hour early, will the room be open? What time will we be finished?—I need to have someone pick me up."

When giving the *location*, be sure to present any directions that may be needed to find it. If finding the place is at all difficult, you'll do better to distribute a map than to try to give directions. Such a map doesn't have to be detailed or complex. A general guide is usually enough. Otherwise, as you try to explain how to get there, you may get interrupted by someone in the audience who will offer a shortcut, an easier way to get there, or correct some detail of yours.

Mention the length of time needed to get there, if appropriate.

In stating the *cost*, consider if you should tell the audience that they have to pay ahead of time, have exact change, can or can't use credit cards, or any other special financial arrangements they may need to know.

If there are *special features*, mention them—but again, briefly. Will baby-sitters be provided? Will buses still be running after the meeting? Are reservations needed in writing? Is there someone to be phoned to get more information?

If there is some special point of *importance* about the subject of your announcement, state it as objectively as you can. You may feel you need to point out that this is the most important meeting of the year, for example. You'll find it more effective to quote someone else— "Our president told me this is really a very important meeting." That's usually better than making your own generalized statement such as, "This one's important."

Finally, are there any *other details* you should mention? Should the audience bring paper and pen, prepare to take notes? Do they have to show their membership cards? Does your announcement apply to everyone in your audience? Should your listeners bring their own materials—perhaps to practice with, show or such? Might the event be moved in case of rain? Or, moved outside if the weather turns out great?

You may remember that back in Chapter Six, when we first introduced you to the format for a speech, we advised you to limit the number of points in the discussion part of a speech to just two to five for most speeches. But the announcement speech is an exception. Here you might have to present as many as ten or more points. But many listeners will just pick out the few points that are important to them. One may remember the date—he's got a birthday that day, so now has to decide if the event you're announcing should compete with that celebration. Another listener may focus on the time—she works late, now has to figure out how to get off early to attend what you're announcing.

The *review,* too, should be brief. All you need to say is something right to the point. For example: "So the trip leaves at 8 AM, Friday, October 2nd, from in front of this building."

The *memorable statement* can be as short as:

See you then.

Hope you'll join us.

Your contribution will be very welcome.

There's no need for you to conclude an announcement with a stirring appeal. Like the cop said so often on that pioneer TV show, *Dragnet,* "Just the facts!"

Here are some additional TIPS for making an effective announcement.

1. Don't give a sales talk.

In a sales talk, you use persuasion techniques; you try to get your audience to buy, agree, vote, attend, whatever. You emphasize benefits, values, needs. But in an announcement, you're simply making the event, situation, or such known to your listeners. You're letting them make up their own minds about whether or not to take part.

2. Prepare and use a note card.

Sure, a note card usually is not appropriate for many speeches as short as an announcement should be. But you need to be sure you state each fact correctly. You need to safeguard against such fumbles as I heard a speaker deliver recently:

The date of our next meeting will be—well, let's see—I said it's the Tuesday after next week, and to-day is . . . what is today's date? Oh, I guess this is the 14th, so that day, Tuesday, not the next one, that would be what?—the 20th? Anyway, it's not that one—it's the Tuesday *after* that, which would be the . . .

By then, the audience was completely confused. They no longer cared. A note card can help you remember your facts and help you state them correctly the first time you give them.

3. Step up to the lectern, platform, or front of the audience with confidence.

How you appear to your audience is important in this speech. Many people do not bother to listen when they know an announcement is to be made. They figure they'll read about it in the club newsletter. Or someone will phone to tell them about the event. Or a friend will remember the details. But you can change that for many of your listeners just by your bearing.

Appear to be confident. Look like you're in charge. Step up with assurance.

Then wait. Don't say a word until you have everyone's attention. That waiting seems like an eternity to many speakers. But you just keep on waiting till everyone settles down. Wait until they are ready to listen to you. It may take a while. That's OK—there's no point in you talking when many in your audience are not yet ready to listen to you. Wait.

Finally, when all is quiet, start to speak. Generally, a slow, quiet delivery is best. That helps rivet attention. It makes people have to listen carefully, intently, to hear what you have to say. That's especially effective in a short speech such as an announcement.

4. Watch out for picky questions.

Questions after an announcement speech can become a problem. Once someone asks one question, others tend to follow along seeking other details. Often the questions are about minor and unrelated points. "If I can't come, can I send someone else? Suppose that other committee decides to meet—then what do we do? If . . . If . . . If . . ." They can go on and on.

To block them, try to be sure you cover every essential point. To check that, you might try your announcement on someone else before you give it to that audience. Often it is helpful to say something such as, "If you have any questions, please see me after this meeting."

For more tips on answering questions, see Chapter Nineteen.

5. Consider using humor.

We've given you several examples in this chapter. Your humor doesn't have to be set jokes. Brief, clever —you hope!—unusual word combinations can add a bit of life to your announcements. Use your own personality. If you've got a way with words, go. If you're uncomfortable using humor, forget it.

6. Consider using a visual aid.

It often helps to hold up a chart with the key facts written large enough so everyone can see. Or if a chalkboard, overhead projector, or other aid is available, you can write facts on there quickly, easily. The visual repeating of your spoken words will help your listeners remember the facts.

7. Be brief.

I know we've already made this point. But it's repeated because so many announcements become so very, very long. Again, TV spots can be a good guide. Notice how to-the-point most of them are.

CHECKPOINTS:
ANNOUNCEMENT SPEECH

As you plan announcements, check off each item below to insure you're ready.

_____ 1. Follow this pattern:

FORMAT FOR ANNOUNCEMENT SPEECH

_____ I. Introduction
   _____ A. Attention-getter
   _____ B. Preview
_____ II. Discussion
   _____ A. Name of event
   _____ B. Date and day
   _____ C. Time
   _____ D. Location
   _____ E. Cost
   _____ F. Special features
   _____ G. Importance
   _____ H. Other details as needed
_____ III. Conclusion
   _____ A. Review
   _____ B. Memorable statement

_____ 2. Change the order of the discussion points as appropriate.

_____ 3. Follow these tips:
   _____ (1) Don't give a sales talk.
   _____ (2) Prepare and use a note card.
   _____ (3) Step up to speak with confidence.
   _____ (4) Watch out for picky questions.
   _____ (5) Consider using humor.
   _____ (6) Consider using a visual aid.
   _____ (7) Be brief.

14

Presenting an Award

> *To speak much is one thing,*
> *to speak well another.*
>
> SOPHOCLES

TODAY, MORE AWARDS are being presented than ever before. There are about 300 manufacturers of trophies, plaques, medals, cups, and other mementos of achievement. They are sold through nearly 6,000 stores, according to the Trophy Dealers of America. A spokesman for that organization, Don Neer, says, "Awards used to be seasonal—now they're year-round."

Many of those awards are presented by someone giving a speech. As the number of awards increase, the chances of you giving a presentation speech are growing, too. You might present a twenty-five-year service pin to a foreman. Or give a certificate of achievement to a production team. Or present a scholarship to a student, a cup to a winning team, or a memento to a visiting dignitary.

Part of the problem in giving this speech is that so many of us see so many fumbles during the telecasts of such award presentations as the Oscars, Tonys, Emmys, even the Patsys—the awards to the outstanding acting by animal actors.

You know the routine. Glamorous actress in low-cut gown comes down a flight of glittering stairs, meets macho actor in a ruffled tux at a chrome-covered speaker's stand. They exchange "clever"—"impromptu"—remarks that a team of writers has been preparing for weeks. Then to the presentation speech. She says, "It's an honor to give this award." He reads the names of a couple of nominees, then she reads the rest. He says, "Here's the envelope." She says, "The winner is . . ."

But that's in the never-never land of television. In the real world you and I live in, presentation speeches need to be much more moving, effective, well-structured.

"You need more tact in the dangerous art of giving presents than in any other social action." That's the claim of British author William Bolitho. He wrote that back in 1929. Yet today, speech professors are often asked, "How do you give a good presentation speech?"

That question's usually asked because of a lack of understanding of the purpose of a presentation speech. It's more than just getting the award to the recipient. If that was all it was, you could have sent the award by mail.

The main purpose is to honor the recipient. That's why the presenting is done in public, through a speech. "Obviously!" sneers the detractor.

But think for a moment. Think of all those poorly presented awards you've seen. Many go wrong because the presenter talked more about the group than the winner. Others miss by building up the award, not the recipient. Some speakers use the occasion to push their own views—sometimes views which have little to do with the award. Indeed, two recent telecast Emmy awards were tarnished by stars pushing political views rather than the point of the event—to honor creative achievements.

The second purpose of a presentation speech is to officially deliver the award. That, too, should be obvious. Yet I've attended award ceremonies in which the presenter had to say, "Well, I don't really have anything to give you, because the cup you were to get didn't arrive." In such a case, present at the very least a piece of paper that says the award is coming. At an award ceremony, certainly, the recipient should receive something. Officially.

The third, the final, purpose of a presentation is to give the recipient an opportunity to express thanks. It's an occasion which many recipients look forward to. This is especially true at retirements, changes of leadership, or other times of significant change. How to give speeches accepting awards is detailed in the next chapter.

A presentation speech should be short. It should follow our established format for a speech, with five special points in the discussion.

FORMAT FOR A PRESENTATION SPEECH

I. Introduction
  A. Attention-getter
  B. Preview
II. Discussion
  A. Purpose of the award
  B. Background of the organization
  C. Review of previous recipients
  D. Brief about current recipient
  E. Description of the award
III. Conclusion
  A. Review
  B. Memorable statement:
    the presentation

"That's a lot to cover in a short speech!" you say? Not really. Each point can consist of but a few sentences. And the format can be adapted as the situation suggests. For example, if it's the first of what is to be an annual award, the purpose would probably be emphasized, so that interest is developed for the future presentations. If the current recipient is especially worthy, you might give more details about him or her.

For the *attention-getter,* try to say something *other* than the old, tired standby lines such as:

It is indeed an honor to make this presentation.

This award is most significant.

We are certainly privileged to be here this evening.

This award goes to the finest person on our staff.

Just as you'd do for your other speeches, go through all the material you might say and pick out the most unusual, interesting, stimulating point. You might say:

Just three years ago, the person who is about to receive this award didn't even know how to keep score in the competition he's now won.

The woman who was the first winner of this award went directly from the ceremonies at which she was presented this honor to the White House to be sworn in as a member of the President's cabinet.

The financial award we're presenting this evening has grown to more than four times the amount of the first award, made just five years ago.

The *preview:*
After your brief attention-getter, move to a short preview of your speech. That can be as simple as:

Tonight, we honor one of our first members.

This award is being presented to one whom we all admire most highly.

In these ceremonies, we continue our long tradition of recognizing superior service in our organization.

The brevity of those statements should be continued in the five points of the *discussion.* Although they need not always be organized in this same sequence, the first point is usually a statement of the *purpose of the award.* For example:

In order to provide recognition to the salesperson who achieves the greatest increase in sales, this special award is made.

The purpose of presenting this cup is to provide the members of the winning team with a constant reminder of their great moments on the playing fields of this school.

You might then include, if appropriate, a brief summary of how the recipient of the award is selected. Sometimes a bit about the background of the donor is included. And you might consider answering such questions as:

When was the award first made?

What prompted it?

Why has it been continued?

How are the recipients selected?

Next, a well-designed presentation speech usually includes—again, very briefly—some words about the *background of the organization* making the award. You might tell the audience how the group started, its purposes, a bit about membership, and a brief summary of major activities. The idea is to refresh the memories of present members, and to inform guests who may not know much about the organization. This point of your speech might be stated in such words as these:

When this company was first organized, none of the very few members realized that in just ten short years we'd be leading the state in the production of our new product.

Our club has been fielding teams for twenty-three years now, and for twenty of those years we've been able to make this presentation to one or more players who have been named to the all-league team.

In addition, you might mention when and how the organization began, the purpose of the group, or why the association decided to make the award.

The third point in the discussion part of a presentation speech can be a *review of previous recipients*. Answer such questions as:

Who won last year, or last time?

Who received the award before that?

What are they doing now?

Where are they?

How has the award helped or encouraged previous winners?

What additional achievements did those earlier recipients go on to acquire?

Be specific. Use names. Mention their present positions, accomplishments, or such. Perhaps some of the previous receivers of the award are in the audience; recognize them, perhaps ask them to stand so the audience can acknowledge them.

But a warning: Don't let your words about the previous winners detract from the honoring of the present recipient. Mention those earlier winners, but don't concentrate on them. Don't let them take the spotlight.

Now you've got your audience ready to hear the name of the current recipient of the award you're presenting. Another delicate spot: Do you keep the name of the winner a secret until the last moment? The answer: It depends.

Some award winners are announced in the newspapers, for example, well before the ceremonies at which the award is presented. Clearly, there's then no point to holding the name back during your presentation speech. But if indeed, secrecy has been maintained, you can build a lot of drama and anticipation by how you word this part of your speech.

In either case—a surprise winner or not—now's the time to present a *brief about the current recipient*. This should be the most important part of your presentation speech. And it should be the most interesting to your audience. Present a brief biography of the recipient.

Emphasize the events and achievements which relate to the award. Questions to answer include:

Why was this person selected?

What contributions did he or she make to this group?

What successes, work, skills, or such qualified the person being honored?

Again—excuse, please, the repetition, but it's needed by many who make presentation speeches—be brief. There's no need to tell long, involved stories. If it's an athlete or a team, you don't have to describe every game, every inning. You might pick out one highlight or so, and relate it in just a few sentences. If the award is being made to someone who's been with the organization for say twenty-five years, you don't need to go through a year-by-year report of the recipient's march up the ladder of leadership. Be brief!

Finally, a short but often overlooked point in the presentation speech: a *description of the award*. Many in your audience may not be able to see just what it is you're presenting. Hold the plaque, trophy, whatever, so all in the audience can view it. Read any inscription —word-for-word.

Describe any symbols or decorations, especially those which may have a significant meaning. Not long ago I was present when awards were made to several people who had helped in a rescue at sea. An impressive plaque was presented to each. In the lower corner of the award was what seemed, at first glance, to be just a rather standard, obvious symbol—a small figure of King Neptune, the sailor's fictional ruler of the sea. But a closer look revealed a couple of swimmers in the waters from which Neptune was rising. Few in the audience realized that those tiny figures were to express great significance —they represented those who had been plucked from the seas. Even if the plaque had been passed around the audience to see close up, even if it had been put on display, many viewers would have overlooked that important symbol.

Now you're ready for the conclusion of your presentation speech. You should give a *review*—a brief statement such as these will be enough:

Thus, this award is one of the most important events of all of our year-long activities.

As you can understand, our recipient is indeed deserving of this award.

Finally, the *memorable statement*—the naming of the recipient. Say it clearly. Slowly. With pride. With honor. Don't use this moment to play the role of the old friend, to capitalize on the setting to draw attention to yourself. Except in the most informal situations, this should be a moment of seriousness, of honoring:

Ladies and gentlemen, this year's winner of the award for the design of our most popular new product—Mr. Steve Stockton.

I now ask Miss Lorie Fremont to step up here and accept this cup.

All told, a presentation speech usually should be only three or four minutes long. Often a shorter presentation is appropriate. Occasionally the speech may become a major address—to the winner of an international peace award, for example. But few of us make such presentations.

Note that you don't have to cover all those points, answer all those questions, in every presentation speech. Select as is appropriate for the situation. If you are presenting twenty-four Boy Scouts with sixty-five merit badges—not an unlikely occasion, as one boy will often earn several badges during a year, for example—you, of course, should not make such a detailed speech for each boy. But you could very well make a preliminary speech applicable to all of the recipients. You'd include the points suggested as they apply to all or most of the Scouts. Then you'd make the individual presentations by simply naming each boy in turn, along with listing the badges won.

Avoid these BLUNDERS.

1. *Don't over-praise the receiver.*

If you're presenting an award to the kid who pitched the winning game at the church social, don't describe him as "the finest little athlete in the entire state!" If you're honoring a salesman retiring after thirty years with an international insurance company, don't claim, "he made the insurance game!—This is the guy who is Mr. Insurance worldwide." Instead, offer praise that is realistic, and thereby sincere. It will be much more effective and impressive.

2. *Don't emphasize the dollar value of the award.*

If it's a check, of course, the amount usually has to be mentioned. But don't say, as I heard in one presentation speech, "Folks, I thought you'd like to know that it cost us nearly thirty dollars to buy this cup." Some may think that's too much; others may think it's insufficient. Either way, it's probably not important to the purpose of the award.

3. *Don't mention those who nearly won.*

Except in special situations, talking about those who just missed getting the award can do more harm than good. It can bring hard feelings to some, disappointment to others. Typically, a speaker will mention this when he or she thinks it may spark others to work harder for the award next year. A coach will say, "I'm sorry you just missed on this one, John, but maybe you can really hit it for us next year, and next year you can be up here getting this cup." Besides possibly either over-challenging John or turning him off, consider what the effect might be on the third and subsequent possible winners. To be safe, it's generally better not to mention near-winners.

4. Don't use humor unless you're sure it's appropriate.

Certainly there are award ceremonies at which humor can be used effectively. At the banquet following the duffers' golf classic. At the presentation of the best-dressed at the costume ball.

But be cautious at presentations of scholarships, sales achievements, retirements, and such. A presenter may make what he considers to be gentle jokes about the award, the organization, or the recipient. But both the giver and the receiver may consider such humor to be making light of an award they consider quite serious. Feelings may be hurt. The image of the event may be damaged. If you're in doubt, chances are you'd better play it straight.

In sum, heed the words of French dramatist Pierre Corneille. Three centuries ago he recognized the same problem you face in a presentation speech today: "The manner of giving is worth more than the gift."

CHECKPOINTS:
PRESENTING AN AWARD

As a help in preparing presentation speeches, check these points.

_____ 1. Keep in mind the purpose of these speeches:
      _____ (1) To honor the recipient.
      _____ (2) To officially deliver the award.
      _____ (3) To provide the recipient an opportunity to express thanks.
_____ 2. Be brief.
_____ 3. Follow this structure:

FORMAT FOR A PRESENTATION SPEECH

_____ I. Introduction
      _____ A. Attention-getter
      _____ B. Preview
_____ II. Discussion
      _____ A. Purpose of the award
      _____ B. Background of the organization
      _____ C. Review of previous recipients
      _____ D. Brief about current recipient
      _____ E. Description of the award
_____ III. Conclusion
      _____ A. Review
      _____ B. Memorable statement: the presentation

_____ 4. Avoid these blunders:
      _____ (1) Don't over-praise.
      _____ (2) Don't emphasize the value of the award.
      _____ (3) Don't mention those who nearly won.
      _____ (4) Don't use humor unless you're sure it's appropriate.

15

Accepting an Award

> *Speeches measured by the*
> *hour die with the hour.*
>
> THOMAS JEFFERSON

THIS IS ANOTHER simple, easy speech about which many people worry. Most worry far too much.

For some reason—possibly because of our years of watching those miserable acceptance speeches on TV award shows—many people seem to think that accepting an award calls for a major oration.

Actually, for many acceptance speeches a simple "Thank you" is sufficient. Sometimes you may be moved to say a bit more. Sometimes you should say more. But only in very formal situations do you need to present a structured speech.

Certainly there's seldom a need for all those foolish acceptance speeches we hear on the telecasts of such awards as the Oscar, Tony, and Emmy. The too-long, too-flowers, too-cute acceptances bring us a few laughs. And we smirk at the cute starlet who's been chasing an award by appearing on talk shows repeatedly, then starts her acceptance speech giggling, "OOooohhhh!!—I just never expected to win!!!" She then delivers a polished, obviously rehearsed, long list of thanks to her hairdresser, dance teacher, judo coach, and more. Someday some actor may be honest enough to add, "And thanks to my writer for preparing this acceptance speech."

You can give more effective, more appropriate acceptance speeches.

First, predict when you might be called upon to give such a speech. If you're going to a company banquet and you've just completed thirty years with the firm, chances are high that you'll receive an award and be expected to give a short acceptance speech.

Here's the guide to follow.

BASIC FORMAT FOR ACCEPTANCE SPEECH

I. Introduction
   A. Attention-getter
   B. Preview
II. Discussion
   A. Express sincere appreciation
   B. Praise help and cooperation
      of others if appropriate
   C. State plans for use, display,
      etc. of the award
III. Conclusion
   A. Memorable statement
   B. Conclusion

By now, if you've read the previous chapters of this book, you well know what to say in that introduction. Your *attention-getter,* just as for your other speeches, might be an interesting story, a stimulating question, or one of the other of the ten techniques detailed back in Step #5, "Beginning Your Speech." You might say, for example:

When I first joined this organization, some of you may remember we worked in an old shed down by the railroad tracks. Today . . .

This being the fiftieth presentation of this annual award makes it an especially significant event.

Then present a *preview,* again as you would in your other speeches. For an acceptance speech, the preview would usually be something as simple and brief as:

I'm moved by your thoughtfulness. Let me speak to you briefly.

Let me say just a few words about why this award is important to our entire organization.

Now move into the discussion part of your speech by expressing your sincere *appreciation* for the award. Again, be brief—*very* brief! Even though this point appears as a major part of the discussion part of your speech, just a sentence or two is usually sufficient.

Next, *praise cooperation and help* you received from other people, if that's appropriate. Despite what we see on TV award shows, there's no need to name a long list of people. Rather, name only those who made a direct contribution to your receiving the award.

If you'll accept a personal example, not long ago I received an award from a Navy group for some writing. In my acceptance speech, I thanked my wife because she does all the proofing—checking the final copy for errors. That's a tough, tedious job. Should I have thanked my barber? He cut my hair during the months I worked on the typewriter. Ridiculous! Thank the deserving. Only.

The third point in the discussion part of your speech should let your audience know of your *plans* for using, displaying, or otherwise utilizing the award. If your award is a check, you might tell your listeners how you intend to use the money. You might say:

These funds will help me continue my studies.

With this check I'll be able to buy the equipment our team needs.

This money will be passed on as a contribution to help the needy families our organization helps support.

If your award is a cup, you might tell the audience:

This cup will take a prominent place on the bookcase in my study.

I'll display this cup in a special case which will be placed in the entry to our office, so all our staff and all our customers can see it.

Where you display it may be significant. I know a magazine publisher who received an award for his magazine—he keeps the award in his home. It should be displayed, several of his writers believe, in the magazine's office, where it might better serve as recognition and stimulation to his staff to continue working for excellence. The point: Make your decision on where to display your award—and what you tell your audience about the display—on the basis of whether the award was given to you for your own personal achievements, or if the award was made to the group which you lead or represent.

Conclude your acceptance speech with a short review. Express again your thanks, your appreciation.

Close with a *memorable statement*. Here are a few examples. Check Chapter Eight for additional ideas.

May I continue to be worthy of this honor.

With this award, our group will now put even more emphasis in continuing the excellence you have honored here this evening.

May the memory of those who have received this award in the past now serve as inspiration to you who are eligible to work for this honor in the future.

What should you say when an award is presented to you as a surprise? You're not expected, then, to come up with a formal speech as we've just outlined. Again, let your own personality and feeling guide you. Just be yourself. Just say what you feel. Only in formal situations, when you knew ahead of time you'd be receiving a presentation, and when a formal speech of acceptance is appropriate—only then should you prepare and present a structured speech.

What if the situation is indeed quite formal, quite significant? Then, the speech structure suggested could be expanded. You might include a bit of your philosophy or attitude or such that you think led to your being selected for this award. You might talk about the future of the award—its significance, its potential impact on next year's recipients. You might mention previous winners—summarizing their contributions, their achievements, and their effect on your own successes.

But such addresses are seldom needed. If your old college is naming the new gym after you because you paid for most of the building costs, then a formal acceptance would be appropriate. If you receive an international peace award, or are honored by an august body such as a national scientific association, then a formal speech would be fitting. As you can see, for most of us, such situations are pretty rare.

Just a few warnings, but they're important.

1. Accept an award in pretty much the same style, manner, and mood as it was presented.

That is, don't give a heavy, emotional response to a casual, light presentation. On the other hand, when the award is presented with dignity and seriousness, don't accept with a couple of flip wisecracks. Indeed:

2. Unless it's a gag award, humor is rarely appropriate.

Almost always, people making an award do so with considerable seriousness. They—the presenter and the audience—will probably be upset if you accept their seriousness with a humorous response. Even a touch of humor can be off-putting.

3. Don't make your speech a major oration if the presentation was informal.

As in most social situations, follow the lead of those just before you. Sure, try to do better than they—try to give a better speech than the presenter. But don't give a lengthy, flowery, elaborate, formal address in accepting an award presented in casual, informal words.

4. Don't worry about this speech!

That's the key to a successful acceptance speech. You rarely have to give one. When you do, the audience seldom expects a major address from you. Relax and enjoy your award. Sit back and relish all those individual "Congratulations!" your friends will be showering on you. Don't let yourself be distracted with worry about what you should say—enjoy!

CHECKPOINTS:
ACCEPTING AN AWARD

If you're going to a presentation ceremony at which you might receive an award, check off these points before you go.

_____ 1. Be brief.

_____ 2. "Thank you" is often all that's needed or appropriate.

_____ 3. If it's really a quite formal situation, use this:

FORMAT FOR ACCEPTANCE SPEECH

_____ I. Introduction
    _____ A. Attention-getter
    _____ B. Preview
_____ II. Discussion
    _____ A. Express sincere appreciation
    _____ B. Praise help and cooperation of others
    _____ C. State plans for use, display of the award
_____ III. Conclusion
    _____ A. Review
    _____ B. Memorable statement

_____ 4. If the award is a surprise, a few words are enough.

_____ 5. If it's a very formal situation or a very significant award: detailing your philosophy, attitude, etc. that led to being selected for the award might be appropriate.

_____ 6. Avoid these blunders:
    _____ (1) Don't use a different style, manner, or mood than the presentation speech.
    _____ (2) Don't use humor unless you're positive it's appropriate.
    _____ (3) Don't make a major oration.
    _____ (4) Don't worry about this speech!

16

Speaking on Television and Radio

> *Conversation is an art in which a man has all mankind for competitors.*
>
> RALPH WALDO EMERSON

IF YOU'RE PREPARING to take over as anchorperson on a television network news show, you must be far beyond the tips to be offered here.

But if you're one of the many ordinary citizens who may appear on TV only occasionally—perhaps even just once in a lifetime—then this chapter is for you.

The chances of your speaking on TV are indeed increasing. More and more local stations invite listeners to reply to company editorials. Concerned individuals appear on community talk shows. People just like you and your neighbors are going on the air to argue for or against the closing of a school, the opening of a new shopping center, an increase in taxes, a decrease in fire protection. There are panel shows, interview programs, discussions, debates, town-halls-of-the-air, and other radio and television programs on which you may speak.

If you are selected—or you volunteer—to appear on such a show, the following guides can help you present your ideas more effectively.

1. Before you appear, watch or listen to another broadcast of the program you're to be on.

Recently another writer and I were interviewed on a half-hour local program about how to break into print. On the way to the studio he asked me, "You know how this show runs? I've never seen it before."

That's like buying a car without taking a test drive. Hazardous. You'll do far better—getting a car you'll like or getting your ideas across on a broadcast—if you find out what you're getting into before you're too far into the deal.

Tune in to the program you're to appear on, to learn how it's presented. Get an idea of its general tone, feeling, atmosphere. Does it look and sound polished and professional, or does it come across as amateurish? What, specifically, are its strengths and weaknesses? If you weren't appearing on it, would your friends still tune in?

Note how the moderator handles him or herself. Does she ask tough, penetrating questions—as if she's a small-town Barbara Walters? Does he try to make the guest tell more than is appropriate—a local version of Mike Wallace? Or are the questions fair, well-balanced?

Is the guest given enough time to state her views clearly? Or does the moderator cut in with another question before an answer is complete?

Does the host interview like a Howard Cosell—pose long, involved questions, use big words, show off his knowledge of your subject? Or is the host a charmer—a Phil Donahue, who becomes the guest's pal, by sympathizing, kidding, showering attention equally on the world-famous actress and the unknown truck driver?

How might such evaluation of a program you're to appear on help you? Certainly there's little or nothing you can do to change the program itself. But you might do a few things to make yourself appear at your best.

If you're to be on a radio program, listen to the

quality of the sound. If it sounds hollow, almost echoing, you'll probably be speaking in a rather large studio, perhaps sitting around a good-sized table. The host may be some distance from you. That may make it difficult to talk conversationally, which is radio at its best. You should try to sit as close as you can to the other people on a radio program.

If you're to be on a TV program, study the set. What's the scenery behind the speakers? One program I was interviewed on had a set which looked like a living room with bookcases in the background. The cover on one book was silver. When a camera got in a particular position, light reflected from the book into the camera. Viewers at home were distracted.

While there's probably little you can—or should— do about such details, they tell you that production of the program is not as careful as it might be. So you need to be as prepared as you can so you, at least, will look and sound your best.

Watch the camera angles. Are they creative or routine? Some shows simply place two cameras before the guest and host, then operate them remotely—from the control room—routinely switching back and forth as the host and then the guest speaks. Better programs move the cameras around—sometimes viewing a speaker head-on, other times through over-the-shoulder shots, showing listeners how the guest looks from the eyes of the host, for example.

Finally, note the colors of the set. They can help you:

2. Select your clothes carefully.

Avoid wearing checks. Seen on TV, big checks may look like a board for a children's game. Small checks may fuzz or appear to vibrate when viewed on home TV sets.

Avoid whites. A white shirt under a navy-blue jacket can make a line where they join, which appears on TV to blur or pulsate.

Jewelry can be distracting, too. It may pick up the

bright studio lights, appear to bounce tiny spotlights into the cameras. Viewed on the typical TV receiver, those spots can turn attention away from what you're saying.

Sammy Davis, some critics claim, wears so much jewelry just so those TV lights will flash off his fingers and his neck. But his jewelry has been a major part of his shtick—his show-business image. Unless you have, or want to project, a similar personality, keep jewelry to a minimum.

Patent-leather shoes, or other shiny shoes, can also pick up studio lights and flash them back into the eyes of viewers. Recently I saw a TV program on which the guest wore such shoes and kept wiggling his feet, apparently to release his nerves. But his moving feet sent shots of light into the cameras, making his shoes more interesting than his speech.

Don't wear ties or scarfs with tiny or mixed patterns, or ones which have strong color contrasts.

So what should you wear? Solid colors are usually best. Wear a light blue shirt or blouse, rather than a white one. A dark blue jacket looks good on TV. So do light brown and tans. Wear ties or scarfs to add solid blocks of complimenting colors.

Best tip: Study what the host on your program wears. Then follow his or her lead. Dress in somewhat the same style. But don't show up looking like a carbon copy. And don't follow the host's clothes to the extent that you end up wearing something that is not your own style.

Also, don't wear clothes which may distract from the point you're to make. If you're speaking on the need to clean up your city's streets, don't show up in torn jeans, a tired T-shirt, and dirty sneakers. That may be your style, but you'll have a hard time convincing your viewers that you're serious about your concern for those dirty streets.

3. *If you're replying to a station's editorial, or broadcasting some other type of set speech, write out what you want to say.*

True, this guide is opposite to the advice presented earlier in this book, that you should not prepare a script for your speeches. But this is a special speaking situation.

Speeches on TV and radio must be timed to exact lengths. When a TV station invites viewers to present one-minute rebuttals to its editorials, those replies must certainly be no shorter than fifty-five seconds, no longer than sixty-five seconds. That may seem restrictive—a mere ten-second leeway. But that's seventeen percent of the time allowed. Timing must be precise so the station can fit the editorials in between the exactly timed programs aired before and after the statements.

To get your broadcast speeches to such precise lengths, it's best to write out what you want to say. Most of us speak faster when under the pressure of the usual studio situation. For a one-minute statement you should usually prepare about sixty-five or seventy seconds.

Another way to insure your broadcast speech will be the correct length is to include, say, two or three short sentences that you can include or drop as the timing requires. If you write such sentences in various places in your speech—rather than having them all in one spot, in sequence—you should be able to include them or drop them without destroying the structure or clarity of your complete statement. You might drop one sentence presenting a statistic, or a short comparison, or a brief example.

Now, what do you do with that full script? If your speech is but a minute or so in length, it should be easy to memorize. But a memorized speech is hard to deliver with enthusiasm and sincerity. So you'll have to work a bit harder on those qualities.

Or, you could write your statement on *idiot cards*.

Those are pieces of cardboard about two-by-three-feet in size, on which you write your speech in large letters. Someone holds these cards quite close to the camera, so you can see them as you give the speech, but they are just outside the range of the camera, so the audience doesn't see them. The typical local station usually won't have anyone around who can hold these cards for you, so you should bring a friend to help.

Or, you might ask the program coordinator, or whoever at the station arranges for your appearance, if you can use a *teleprompter*. That's a mechanical device which fits onto a TV camera. Your speech is typed on a long roll of paper, using a special machine which types letters about three-quarters of an inch high. The machine moves this paper before you as you speak, so you can read your words as you look into the camera. But getting a teleprompter ready takes some time of the station's staff, so few local shows use them for such speeches.

Your final option: Simply have your speech in hand and read it. That's not necessarily poor delivery. Know your speech well enough so you don't have to look at your script all the time. Rather, practice enough so you can just look now and then to remind yourself of an occasional sentence or thought.

4. If you're speaking on an interview show, panel, or such program, don't prepare particular answers to specific questions.

This will make the program sound quite artificial. Besides, you'll rarely get the host to ask the questions just as you want.

Rather, know your subject thoroughly. Usually you'll meet with the host of the program about a half-hour before air time. He or she will talk with you informally to set you at ease and to become a bit familiar with how you speak—your style, enthusiasm, fluency, and such.

Almost always the host will give you an idea of what will be asked of you. He or she might say, for example, "I'll be asking you how you got interested in this problem. And we'll want to know how you recommend this be solved."

Sometimes you'll also be asked if there are any particular points you want to talk about or questions which you want asked of you. You should prepare for that by taking this next step:

5. For the host, type on a card a very short list of ideas you want to talk about.

That card will be greatly appreciated by most radio and TV hosts. Don't feel you're being a show-off in doing this. Rather, you're helping the host structure the program. And you're helping yourself tend to insure you'll get to present the ideas you want to.

Usually it's best to type the information on a three-by-five-inch card. Type on one side only. Double space. The statements—not questions—should be brief enough so they'll fit on one card. Here's a sample:

```
Need for community cleanup:
  1. State survey named our town
     "least desirable to live in."
  2. Our garbage is collected less
     frequently than in any nearby
     town.
  3. All street sweeping stopped
     after last year's tax cuts.
```

The points should be just a few. They should be quite specific. You're hoping the host will use them as the basis for questions asked of you on the air.

6. Type on another card information the host can use to introduce you.

Include only information which relates directly to the topic you're presenting on the program. Don't prepare a long list of all your activities or interests. A helpful card would look like this:

```
Nancy Brent:
    Chairman of the Community Cleanup
       Committee.
    Resident of this city for fifteen
       years.
    Leads a group of more than fifty
       concerned citizens.
```

Note the brevity. The first point should usually be your title or some other statement which may establish your authority, experience, concern, or involvement in the topic of the program. The next statement might show how or why you're informed about the topic. Then you might include a line that shows others are concerned, or have studied the topic, or are working on the problem—to get your viewers thinking of how widespread interest is in the problem.

Soon, now, your host will be moving you into the studio from which you'll broadcast. A studio, especially a TV studio, is usually a very busy place indeed. But you should:

7. Ignore the action in the studio.

For many people not in broadcasting, their first look into a TV studio can be almost overwhelming. The varied, intensive activity to get a show on the air impresses almost all outsiders.

One of the crew may be adjusting lights. Another checks the microphones. A cameraman opens the side of a camera, screwdriver in hand, making adjustments. The director's voice will come over a sound system— "Five minutes to air!" Someone may check the large clock placed just off-camera, but in view of the host. A sound person or the host may clip a tiny mike to your jacket. From the studio you may look through a glass partition, see technicians in the control room operating a swarm of switches, monitoring a mass of meters.

A graphics specialist may come in, ask the host for your name so she can type it into the character-generator—the machine which makes those electronic titles you see superimposed over a speaker's picture.

All this, and more, may be going on all around you. Ignore it.

Ignore everything and everyone. Except your host. And the floor manager—she may tell you something such as, "Move your chair a little to the right, would you, please?"

The action may seem like desperate last-minute efforts to get your show on the air. Actually, in almost all studios, the staff schedules—rather than delays—details to be done just before air time. Remember that the program you are on is not the only show on the air. The staff has been busy working on the program before yours, and also must get ready for the show which follows. Even if those other programs are on film, tape, or network feeds—programs which come from another station—the staff has work to do on them.

So don't worry. Trust the studio staff. They know what they're doing. You should try to relax and get your own mind and appearance ready to air.

8. Decide who you're going to talk with—the host only or the TV audience, too.

You have two possibilities. You can talk only with your host and any other guests who may be on the program. That gives viewers the impression they're looking in on the conversation. Or, you can look into the on-the-air-camera. That makes viewers feel they are included in the talk.

Which is better? It depends on the image you want to convey. Both are effective. The best solution—ask your host, "Do you want me to look at you, or at the cameras?"

But getting your eye to catch the right camera at the right moment can be difficult. The cameras are switched from one to another, by the director. He or she is in the control room, not the studio where you're talking. When a camera is turned on, a red light shines from the top of that camera. It takes some skill to pick out the correct camera to look into while also concentrating on what you're saying. It's much easier to just forget the cameras and talk with your host and the other guests.

Just as you look into one camera, the director might decide to cut to another. Professionals, such as the typical guest on a Carson show, train on how to pick out the on-air camera. Sometimes a floor manager helps by standing out-of-view, between cameras, pointing to a camera just as it is turned on. If the speaker is sharp enough to watch for those signals and at the same time keep track of what he or she's saying, then the viewer can feel involved in the program.

The Dick Cavett show generally follows the other technique. Except for the opening, Cavett looks into the camera only occasionally. Most of his guests seldom look at a camera. They just talk to each other and to Cavett. The viewer is, in effect, listening in, rather than taking part.

Therefore:

9. Decide if you're going to try to chase the on-air cameras.

If you're not experienced in picking out the on-the-air camera, the one with a red light shining, you'll do better to just forget the cameras and talk with the people on the program.

In any event, don't expect a station—local or network—to take time and staff to practice with you so you can pick out the on-air camera.

10. Consider the on-air camera or microphone as just another individual you're talking with.

If you should decide to try to keep track of which camera is telecasting—that is, if you are going to include the audience in the conversation you're having with the host—then the next step is to mentally consider the camera, or microphone, as someone you're talking with.

Some TV performers do that by picturing a specific person to be the camera or mike. The imagined person might be a real individual—a spouse, friend, parent, or such. Other TV personalities picture a "Mr. or Ms. Average"—a composite of the typical viewer they think is tuned to the program.

I don't find having an imagined person—real or composite—helpful to me. I just look at the camera now and then, or at the microphone when on radio. No mental picture. No invented image. I realize there is another person, or maybe a few, out there at the end of that equipment. But I concentrate more on what I'm saying and how I say it. I look on it as though the host, that camera or mike, and I are having a nice three-way conversation.

11. Be yourself.

Sure, you've read that repeatedly in this book. But it's even more important when you're on TV or radio. They are very intimate, close-up mediums. It's hard to lie on TV—the camera catches that flutter of your eye, that extra bit of air your lungs grasp. Radio emphasizes

your sighs, your pauses, your change of vocal qualities.
"I'm not going to lie!" you reply. But many people
go on TV planning to . . . well, enhance their images a
bit. A friend of mine, a writer, takes on a slight British
accent when he's on TV—apparently he feels he needs
to sound a bit more cultured! Clearly, a great many
politicians and bureaucrats come on TV and radio
speaking in a language that's filled with long words,
obscure phrases, and wandering sentences. Attempts to
sound more important that you are, or to try to build
a minor event into something big is, in effect, lying.
And that's difficult to do with sincerity before a TV
camera or a radio mike.

12. Realize that you're not speaking to a giant audience, but to individuals.

The program you're on may be broadcast to an audience of thousands, maybe even a million or more viewers or listeners. That may lead you to think, *Wow!—
I'm talking to a really big audience!!*

Well, not exactly. On TV and radio, you communicate with *individuals*. Obviously your giant audience is
not seated together in one big auditorium. Rather,
they're usually at home, seated before their TV sets—
alone, or maybe with one or a few other people. Or they
may be driving along in their cars, radios turned on,
usually alone, perhaps with one or just a few fellow
riders.

Since radio and TV audiences do not tune in as a
group, they do not react as a group. If you had a few
hundred listeners in one room—or even just a few
dozen—your speaking could get them to move each
other to react to your words. A joke that gets a few
people laughing in an in-person audience will spark
others to join in the laughter. But a joke heard on TV
or radio, in the privacy of the viewer's home, for example, will usually produce more of a mental pleasure.
Oh, some in a broadcast audience may smile slightly,

and a rare individual may break out into audible laughter.

Since you're talking with individuals, your speaking techniques should be somewhat different on a broadcast than for an in-person audience. For one thing:

13. *Speak quietly, informally, conversationally.*

Even if you're giving a speech, rather than being interviewed or taking part in a discussion, your style should usually be more casual, personable.

There's no need to speak loudly—the microphone will carry your voice. It will be heard by your listeners almost as if you're chatting with them in a personal, one-to-one conversation.

Your emphasis should not be as strong as when delivering a speech to a live audience. Pauses should be briefer. Inflections should be less on broadcasts.

Your visual presentation should also be adapted to TV and radio. The major technique:

14. *Keep gestures low-key.*

Before a live audience, a sweep of your arm can add impact to what you're saying. On TV, such a broad gesture can appear to be overdramatic, overdone.

When you're on TV, viewers are much closer to you than when you speak before an in-person audience. TV cameras, as you well know, rarely project a full picture of a speaker. Much of the time a speaker is shown from just the shoulders up—a "head shot," TV people call that. Or they telecast a "waist shot," which shows a bit more. On such close-up pictures, the wave of an arm can look like a quarterback throwing a pass.

That difference in gesturing on TV creates a problem for many stage actors and actresses. In a theater, their gestures must carry a message to the last row of the top balcony. Such gestures are forceful, broad, dramatic.

But on the close-up views of television, stage gestures appear artificial.

So, if you gesture when you're on TV, keep your motions small, casual, calm.

What about gesturing on a radio program? "Well, the audience can't see your gestures, so there's no need for them." That's the reply many people give—on first thought.

But think again. On radio, obviously, you have to rely on your voice alone to get your messages across. Gestures, however, can do much to help you add emphasis to your voice. To prove this, visit a radio studio sometime. Watch a disk jockey at work. Sometimes you can stand outside a studio, not hearing the sound, and look in through a glass partition. Almost every radio performer gestures. Many of them gesture wildly, constantly.

So use gestures when you're on a radio program, too. They'll help you punch up your ideas. And gestures will help you relax.

15. Be alert to signals to stop talking.

When you see talk show host John Davidson put his hand on a guest's arm, don't think he's being friendly. Rather, that's a widely used signal in broadcasting. It means, "Finish what you're saying, soon."

That same message is often delivered in the same way by such different hosts as Phil Donahue, Merv Griffin, and Johnny Carson. Barbara Walters tells about her interview on the "Today" program of actor Leo G. Carroll. He's most remembered, probably, for his role on "The Man from U.N.C.L.E." To tell Carroll that time was running out, Walters touched his knee. He didn't get that message. He said, on the air, "Young woman! What are you doing crawling up my thigh!"

When you're on TV, watch your host for such signals. There will also be signals from someone else in the studio, usually the stage manager. He or she may use quite a variety of signals. Some show the minutes and seconds left. Others mean speed up or draw the program out—fill in with additional talk. There are other signals, too. But they are all directed at the host, not you. Ignore them. Take your cues from your interviewer or moderator.

16. Watch other talk shows to improve your skills.

Note how Merv Griffin looks right in the eyes of his guests. That does much to make them more open in what they say. Indeed, stage star Carol Channing once told Griffin that his intense, concentrated involvement makes her say things she didn't intend to say to a national audience.

Observe how Phil Donahue draws out arguments for opposing views by saying such things as, "Well, some people claim your ideas may be wrong because . . ." Watch Carson mug to the camera after giving a guest an apparently clean-cut question which leads to an off-color reply. Watch how Mike Wallace glances at the ceiling, sighs, pats his hands together when he is told a story he finds hard to believe.

While you may not expect to appear on one of those major shows, you can learn much from them. Observe how hosts handle guests. Study how guests respond—some becoming lively, interesting, through expert questioning. Other guests grow defensive, argumentative as an interviewer seems to attack, as shown by some investigative reporters on news and commentary shows. Most important, note how skilled guests keep working in the subject that led them to appear on the program. An author will reply to a question about what she thinks should be done about a problem by saying, "As I explain in Chapter Three of my book, . . ." An ecologist will say, "But let me return to my main idea, that . . ."

Appearing on TV can be a lot of fun. And of course TV gets your ideas to a great many people very quickly. So don't be like some of the students I've had in my classes who, when asked to appear on a television program, beg off with such lines as "Oh, I'm not good enough." Or, "I'd be too scared!" Follow the tips in this book and you should do fine.

CHECKPOINTS:
SPEAKING ON TELEVISION AND RADIO

To appear at your best when on a broadcast, follow these guides.

_____ 1. Before you appear, watch or listen to another broadcast of the program you're to be on.

_____ 2. Select your clothes carefully.

_____ 3. If you're replying to a station's editorial, or broadcasting some other type of set speech, write out what you want to say.

_____ 4. If you're speaking on an interview show, panel, or other such program, don't prepare particular answers to specific questions.

_____ 5. For the host, type on a card a very short list of ideas you want to talk about.

_____ 6. Type on another card information the host can use to introduce you.

_____ 7. Ignore the action in the studio.

_____ 8. Decide who you're going to talk with—the host only, or the TV audience, too.

_____ 9. Decide if you're going to try to chase the on-air camera.

_____ 10. Consider the on-air camera or microphone as just another individual you're talking with.

_____ 11. Be yourself.

_____ 12. Realize that you're not speaking to a giant audience, but to individuals.

_____ 13. Speak quietly, informally, conversationally.

_____ 14. Keep gestures low-key.

_____ 15. Be alert to signals to stop talking.

_____ 16. Study other talk shows to improve your skills.

17

Checking Arrangements

> *As a vessel is known by the sound whether it be cracked or not, so men are proved, by their speeches, whether they be wise or foolish.*
>
> DEMOSTHENES

ONE TIME I was the speech writer for the Navy's admiral in charge of research. He was to make a speech to about twenty congressional leaders. Our checking of the arrangements included:

* A search through about twelve Navy commands in Norfolk, Virginia, to find the two top projectionists and the two top sound technicians, then getting them transferred to our staff for a week, to check and operate the equipment used with the admiral's speech.
* A detailed, two-hour inspection, two weeks before the speech, by a Captain, a Lieutenant Commander, and two technicians, of the room in which the speech was to be made.
* Flying, a day ahead of time, a crew of about a dozen to Washington, D.C.—where the admiral would give his speech.
* A six-hour dress rehearsal.

* Setting a two-man all-night guard on the room and its equipment, to make sure no projector was moved, no microphone lowered.

You don't have to check arrangements for your speeches that carefully. Well, not usually. Still, it is wise to take *some* precautions.

And if you're like most of us who give speeches— that is, if you have fewer assistants than an admiral— there's one basic guide: *DO IT YOURSELF!*

Don't count on someone else to make sure all the details for your speech are as *you* want them. Unless you give very precise instructions, that other person will check arrangements so they'll meet his standards, not yours. He may remember to make sure there's a glass of water on a table near the speaker's position— but you'd have to tell him that you usually drink several glassfuls, so there should also be a pitcher filled with water.

A problem in arrangements I face comes when I speak to a group of, say, thirty or fewer listeners. For such a small audience, I like to perch on a stool. Just a regular, old-fashioned stool. The kind that is in many kitchens. But such a stool is seldom found in a classroom, or meeting hall, or the other places people gather to hear speeches. So if I want a stool, I could ask whoever invited me to speak to be sure there's one available. But often I get a box. Or a piano stool. Or a chair. Or a few hours before I'm to speak I get a phone call and the moderator asks, "Will a small bench do?" "How about a low stepladder?" Or he says, "We're having trouble finding a stool—but I think we can get one from across town. Shall I have someone get it, or can you get along without one?"

It's easier to bring my own!

Now many people will read that example and think, *What a picky guy this speaker is!* But you, too, may have some little details that will help make your speaking situation into the best you can to help you give an effective speech.

If you speak fairly often, it may be worth your while

to add to the list of checkpoints at the end of this chapter any special items you'd like to have arranged for your speech. To start that list, here are arrangements many speakers check on before speaking.

1. Parking

More than one speaker has arrived a "safe" fifteen minutes before speaking, only to find that parking is in a lot several blocks away. Hiking back to the hall, arriving at least a bit out of breath, such speakers fail to give themselves time to collect their thoughts, to take in the feeling of the room and the mood of their listeners.

Try to arrange for parking without sounding like a self-appointed star. Ask if there might be a reserved parking space for your car. If you have audio or visual aids you'll be using in your speech—even an easy-to-carry box of slides—you might use the delivery of them to get a space reserved. Or try to talk your way past any security guard who might be around—"I'm the guest speaker—I've got some gear to take in. Parking next to the stage door's OK for the speaker—right?"

At the very least, find out what arrangements there are for parking. Best: If possible, a few days ahead of time, drive past the building where you're to speak, to note if parking is accessible. Or, ask someone—the chairman, program arranger, president of the group—where she suggests you park.

Consider parking, say, a mile or so away and taking a taxi. That will usually cost but a few dollars, and should get you there promptly. And if you rarely take a taxi, that can add a valuable bit to your self-image—making you feel somewhat important, and thereby possibly improving your confidence in speaking.

2. Lectern

Lecterns can be mighty impressive structures. Many are massive, sturdy, ornate. They look like they're built by the same guy who did gun towers for old castles. The intent, of course, is to make the speaker behind the lectern look authoritative.

But most lecterns are built for tall speakers. A short person trying to make eye contact with his audience when speaking from behind the typical lectern has a problem. Peering over the top, he or she looks like a kid trying to sneak a peek at Christmas presents.

Some lecterns have a little box set inside, perhaps four inches high. Short speakers are expected to move that box into position, then stand on it, so they'll appear taller. Well, that sounds like a good idea. But often the box is awkward to move into place. You have to bend over, disappear entirely behind that lectern. If you try to kick that box into place, you may find it's hinged, and you end up with a scuffed shoe, perhaps a tender toe. The point, in noting such details, is that for most of us, the moment we get up to speak we don't want to have to be bothered—nervous as we are with a million or more other thoughts—with a lectern that makes us look or feel uncomfortable.

That's why you're urged to check out this and other such arrangements well before you step up to speak.

3. Seating

Fletcher's first rule of audiences says:

The bigger the room and the smaller the audience, the farther they'll sit toward the back of the room.

That makes it difficult for the speaker. You don't want rows of empty chairs between you and your listeners. You'll feel uncomfortable, unwanted.

Once listeners settle into those seats far away from

the speaker, they quickly become firmly attached to them. They get possessive. They don't want to move. Most of all, they don't want to be asked to move!

What's a speaker to do?

Plan ahead. A few days before your speech, visit the room in which you're to speak. Make a good guess of how many people will come. If the room will seat many more than you expect, arrive about an hour before your speech, tape a ribbon, or crepe paper, or such, to block entry to the back rows of seats. As more people show up, remove the tape from more rows.

If you didn't plan ahead, if you arrive for your speech and find just a few people sitting far away from the speaker's position, then *you* should move to be near your audience. You can speak while standing between a couple of rows just in front of them. Or you might stand in the aisle to give your speech. In any event, don't let there be a big, empty space between you and your listeners.

But whatever you do, *don't* ask your audience to "move down to these front seats." Just last week I attended a church service in which the chapel was only about one-quarter filled. Most people were sitting at the back. Services included a small group singing quiet songs, accompanied by a soft-sounding guitar. The minister said, "Let's all move forward so we're sitting in the front twelve rows." My daughter immediately started counting the rows in front of us. We were winners!— we were seated in the twelfth row. As others moved from behind us, I noticed many who appeared unhappy at being moved out of the seats in which they had quickly come to feel at ease.

Once a speaker asks listeners to move, he's usually forced some degree of hostility on them. Most will move, but they won't like it. Many will not move. Some will remain unhappy—whether they moved or not—for much, possibly all, of the speech. This can be especially damaging to a speaker who is trying to argue a viewpoint, present a new proposal, or sell something.

There is another solution. If there are just a few people in the audience—say twenty or so—it's usually best to have them seated informally, in an arc of, say, just two rows. Or, consider seating in a circle, with you a member of that circle, not in the middle.

But in making such a decision, consider, again, the purpose of your speech. If you're about to give a group of, say, twelve employees a new set of strict rules, a more formal seating may be more appropriate. If you expect your listeners to take notes, try to get your speech scheduled in a room which has chairs with table-arms, as in many lecture halls—both large and small—in many modern schools.

The main point: Seating can help or hinder your speech. Don't blow your speech over a detail you can prevent from becoming a problem by just a little advance planning.

4. Sound system

I've got a speaker's rule about sound systems, too:

The more times a speaker is told 'the sound system is no problem,' the more likely it is to be a problem.

The two most frequent problems:

1. Raising or lowering the microphone.
2. Controlling the system—the volume and the feedback, that howling sound when the thing starts acting up.

For specific suggestions on how to solve those and other such problems, see the next chapter. A little thing like a sound system shouldn't deserve a full chapter, except for the fact that these outfits can—and do!—interfere seriously with the success of many speeches.

The essential point here is to check the public address system well before you give your speech.

5. Audiovisual aids

If you're going to show slides, run a film, or use any other kind of audio or visual aids with your speech, check the arrangements. Then check again! And *again!!*

To be safe, you should get your aids set in place and operating some three or four hours before your speech. That will give you time to run down to a hardware store to get an extension cord when the only wall plug is too far away for the cord that comes with the projector. You say, "But there should be an extra extension cord in the hall!" You're right. But often there isn't. Or it's locked up in a closet. And the guy with the keys has the day off. Or a million or more other problems can arise.

Most dangerous of all can be an offer such as, "Oh, you can use our projector—I'm sure it can handle your slides." The more positive the moderator is in saying something like that, the more likely it is that the equipment doesn't match. Or won't work. Or is out on loan. Or some other such problem develops.

Often such a moderator will not bother to get other equipment. Usually he'll brush the problem aside by saying something such as, "Well, they told me you're a good speaker—so you should be able to give just as good a talk without using those visual aids." And there go your weeks of collecting and arranging slides. There goes that dramatic presenting of your points in an outline visual. There goes the speech you planned, and here comes a nearly impromptu talk!

Don't trust arrangements for audiovisual aids to anyone other than yourself! And give yourself plenty—plenty!—of time to solve problems that may arise. Finally, check the equipment yourself *before* you speak. If it is defective, and there is no time to fix it, be prepared with some other way of presenting your material.

6. Water

I *never* get a cough when speaking. Except when I give a speech when I've forgotten to bring cough drops!

That's the time there's no water ready for the speaker. Then just a tiny tickle develops. It starts as soon as I notice there's no water. As I check my pockets for cough drops, the problem in my throat increases. The more pockets I find empty, the faster comes the cough. The bigger the audience, the more important the speech, the greater the urge to cough. Most of the time I don't actually cough—I just feel like I'm about to.

That cough is, of course, merely mental. Worry about coughing and chances are greater that you will cough. Find no water for the speaker and chances are increased that you'll feel like coughing.

So, when checking arrangements for your speech, block that mental cough by making sure there's water. And a glass. And a pitcher with more water. Without a pitcher, someone else may come up and drink the entire glass of water in one gulp. Or someone with a deathly hack will cough all over the glass, making you feel you'll catch a disease if you even look at the glass. And then, another tickle will start in your throat.

7. The introduction of you.

It's irritating to listen to someone fumble your name as you're introduced, or to give your title incorrectly. Or say you work for a company that's a competitor. Or listen to all the other mistakes a chairman can make.

But besides being bothersome, such goofs can destroy the opening of your speech. Rather than starting out with that great attention-getter you planned, your first words have to correct the mistakes spoken by your introducer. That can confuse your listeners. And it might get them giggling at the start of a speech you planned to open in a serious tone.

To avoid such hazards, type on a card a few bits of information about yourself which the chairman can use to introduce you to your listeners. The card should be like the one we suggested in Chapter Sixteen that you give to the host of a TV or radio program. A sample card is included there. It should be brief—your name, title, and a few facts about you which document your knowledge or experience in the subject of your speech.

It's a good idea to mail this card to whomever is to introduce you. It should be sent so it will arrive a week or so before you speak. Some speakers have in their files a page or two summarizing their qualifications, experiences, education, and such. It can help to send a copy of that, too, to your introducer. But if you send it only, and not the card with the essential points to introduce you, then you're leaving it up to the introducer to select from your more complete listing the points to introduce you. He or she may select items that don't relate to the topic of your speech. So it's safer if you prepare a card with the key points you prefer to be said about you.

In addition to mailing a card to the introducer, bring another copy of the card to the meeting at which you're to speak. Too often a moderator will ask a speaker just before she's on, "Anything special you want me to say to introduce you?" He's forgotten to bring that card you prepared so carefully!

8. How questions will be handled.

In Chapter Nineteen you'll get specific tips on how to answer questions. Our concerns here are the details you should work out with the chairman, moderator, or whomever introduces you, so the question period will be conducted efficiently.

Of course questioning does not follow every speech. But if you're giving a talk urging action, proposing a change, or on any argumentative subject, your listeners should be given an opportunity to ask questions. Not providing for questions after such speeches may lead some listeners to believe that you're either covering up some information or you're afraid to answer questions.

The easiest—and often best—arrangement is simply to lead the question period yourself. Then you're in control of the situation. The chairman may be able to lead the questions as well as you can, maybe even better. But there is the possibility that the chairman may be inept—call on one aggressive person several times, let questioners give arguments against your views, even let listeners start arguing among themselves. If you have any doubts whatever about the moderator's skills, lead your own question period.

If the chairman runs the questioning, you can still guide it to be as effective as possible. It's best to work out details before your speech. Unless there are but a few people in the audience, ask the chairman to repeat each question to make sure everyone hears. That will also help make sure you hear the questions correctly. If, after the first couple of questions, you note that the chairman is allowing one person to ask several questions, you can speak up and suggest, "How about that person in the back corner? Let's hear that question."

Another way to conduct the question period is by having slips of paper distributed to your listeners. It's better to have them given out before you speak, so listeners can jot down questions that come to their minds as you speak. Then you or the moderator can collect the questions, have someone else collect them, or have them passed up to you. But there are some disadvantages in this process.

To some listeners, written questions seem to be restricting communications. Some people feel it's a bother to write out a question. Of course, many of them have trouble wording a question in specific terms. But that's one of the advantages of this technique: It gets more questions into more precise wording. Besides, even if you do have questions written out, you can still invite questions called out by your listeners.

One major advantage of written questions is the questioner does not have to identify him or herself. Some people are shy about asking questions. Others may want to ask something that reveals their own views and don't want others to know who asked such a question.

Which is the best procedure? Once again, you should decide on the basis of what you think will be most helpful to your attaining the purpose of your speech. If you want to keep the situation informal and as open as possible, you lead the question period. For greater formality, have the moderator handle the questions. In still more formal speaking situations, written questions are usually submitted.

9. After your speech—what then?

After most of the speeches most of us give, the chairman comes over and gives you a "Thank you" and you're on your own. Frankly, I prefer that. But every once in a while more elaborate activities may be scheduled for you. And you'd better know about them ahead of time!

The first time I gave a speech which was followed by a meeting with the press, I was caught far off-guard. I was already well along into relaxing after hearing that nice applause following my speech. The audience was filing out of the hall. The chairman said I'd done a "fine job"—and then added, "Now, if you'll come with me to this little room just down the hall, we have a number of members of the press who'd like to talk with you." Suddenly my nerves were all charged up again! A few more steps and I'm facing glaring lights and a half-dozen microphones! Behind them, cameras! And news hawks with tough questions, I feared.

Actually, the questions were easy. Chances are, should you get into such a situation, you, too, will find the press friendly. Usually they just want a few statements from you recorded on their TV or radio tapes, or jotted on pads by newspaper reporters, so they can individualize their stories about your speech.

Well, press conferences rarely follow any of the

speeches most of us give. But you can end up in situations far worse.

There might be a reception that you didn't expect. Or a dinner, or a small snack with the officers of the group to which you spoke. Occasionally there's a cocktail party at which you're expected to mix, to talk with a lot of people—many of whom are more interested in getting you to listen to them!

All these activities can be interesting side benefits of speaking. But you'll be more comfortable, handle such events better, if you know about them ahead of time. Sometimes these events aren't planned at the time you are asked to speak; they develop later. But you'd best know about them before you're suddenly in the middle of something like an "intimate little get-together," as one moderator described a party for some fifty people which was sprung on me after one of my speeches.

10. Additional arrangements you may like.

For years, Bob Richards, superior motivational speaker and former Olympic champion, asked that a local track be reserved so he could work out by running a couple of miles before speaking. Another speaker insists a hotel room be provided—free, of course—whether he's speaking on the road or in his hometown. He likes to relax and get "up" for his speeches in such a setting. Another speaker, a writer, asks for a chauffeured limousine to drive him to several bookstores, so he can check the sales of his works.

Very few of us who give speeches need or expect such arrangements. Still, there may be some special details that typical citizens such as you and I may like. If glaring lights hurt your eyes, ask that there be none. If smoking bothers you, ask that it be restricted to outside the room in which you're speaking. If . . .

You get the idea. If you have one or more personal preferences for when you speak—as rare as those speeches may be—you can add them to the checklist on the next page, to make sure you remember to attend to them.

In checking arrangements for your speeches, just as for so many aspects of speaking, the best technique by far is to do as the successful professional speaker—*prepare*. Plan ahead. Then you can control the situation, rather than letting the speaking situation control you.

CHECKPOINTS:
CHECKING ARRANGEMENTS

Use this list to make sure all details have been taken care of in arranging for your speeches.

_____ 1. Parking.
_____ 2. Lectern.
_____ 3. Seating.
_____ 4. Sound system.
_____ 5. Visual aids.
_____ 6. Water.
_____ 7. The introduction of you.
_____ 8. How questions will be handled.
_____ 9. After your speech—what then?
     _____ (1) Party?
     _____ (2) Reception?
     _____ (3) Meeting with officials?
     _____ (4) Press conference?!!?
     _____ (5) Something else?
_____ 10. Additional arrangements you'd like:
     _____ (1) _____
     _____ (2) _____
     _____ (3) _____
     _____ (4) _____

18

Using a Microphone

*In chatter excellent, but
unable quite to speak.*

EUPOLIS

UNTIL ABOUT SEVENTY-FIVE years ago, a speaker, to be heard by an audience of more than about a hundred people, had to be good at "projecting the voice." Projecting is, in a sense, controlled shouting. Public speakers used to do a lot of yelling, roaring, even screaming.

Then, in 1907, Dr. Lee DeForest invented the microphone. That, along with amplifiers, speakers, and other attached equipment, changed public speaking significantly.

No longer did a speaker have to shout at his listeners. Now he or she could cozy up to a microphone, speak softly, personably. Even when speaking to an audience of thousands, he could make each listener feel as though he were listening to a personal, individualized conversation. Public speaking became much closer to one-to-one chats, rather than formal orations to mass audiences. Suddenly a speaker could be much more persuasive. Now he could really "sell" his ideas, information, beliefs.

Today, continued improvements in public address systems have given speakers greater power than ever. You don't even have to switch on some mikes—say something and they turn themselves on, voice-activated.

225

There are radio mikes—wireless mikes—some smaller than a dime. You can clip one of these to your blouse or coat, then walk around as you speak. You'll have no worries about wires getting tangled or your listeners not hearing you. And sound systems—good, modern ones —have virtually eliminated the horrible electronic distractions of clatter, squeals, howls—"feedback."

But there's one major problem. Many speakers fail to realize, even today, the power of a microphone—*when used properly*.

Using a microphone correctly is certainly not difficult or complex. To some speakers, how to use a mike hardly seems worth a chapter in a speech book. Still, there are quite a few simple techniques which many speakers don't know about, or don't remember to use.

1. Check the microphone ahead of time.

How far ahead of time? That depends on how important your speech is to you. And it depends on your guess of how good the sound equipment is in the place you're going to speak.

At the very least, arrive in time so you'll have some fifteen minutes to check the mike. You'll probably also need time to meet a few officials, size up the audience, make a last-minute run to the john. So give yourself plenty of lead time.

To check the mike, first find out how close you have to be to it. Ask the program chairman or whoever is going to introduce you—chances are he or she has used the same mike before. But don't accept a vague reply such as, "Oh, don't worry, just stand up there and it will pick you up." Almost always that means the person you asked doesn't really know, or doesn't know how to use a mike properly.

So ask if there's a technician, custodian, or someone around who sets up or operates the public address system. If there is, take the time to ask him or her.

If there isn't such a person, you certainly should take

the few seconds needed to go up to the speaker's stand and actually try the mike.

Speak into it with your mouth about four to six inches away. Just talk in your usual speaking voice. Don't do what you've seen so many speakers do to check a mike—tap it.

Technicians will tell you, "Never tap a mike!" A good mike can easily be damaged by tapping on it. Furthermore, tapping tells you nothing except whether the mike is "on." You still don't know how far from it you should be while speaking. And that tapping often makes a really uncomfortable booming noise in the ears of listeners. The knowing ones would already tag you as an amateur.

So just say a few words, such as "Good afternoon. Good afternoon—am I being heard clearly?" Many speakers use the old line, "Testing—one, two, three—testing!" That's OK—but many who use it don't deliver it in their usual speaking volume or style, and so, once again, they often learn little more than whether or not the mike is working.

Try speaking—just a few words are enough—a bit farther away from the mike. Try about twelve inches away. Then move in closer to just an inch or so from the mike. Some mikes have a sudden "drop-off"—get more than, say, ten inches away, and they won't pick up your voice at all. Other mikes still pick you up the farther you get from them, but your voice becomes quieter and quieter. Clearly, it's important for you to know this characteristic of the mike you're about to use.

Finally, try the mike while speaking to one side or the other of the audience. Some mikes will pick your voice up only if you speak directly into them. Others will pick you up even when you're talking way off to the side.

Many speakers worry that some people in an audience won't like the checking of the mike. I haven't found that to be true. Oh, occasionally a few people out there want to keep up their own little conversations before the meeting starts and are bothered by mike checking. But your checking will take just a few seconds —unless you find a problem. Besides, many of your listeners may spot you as really knowing what you're doing—you're making sure the equipment is ready for use. No need to worry.

If you do find a problem, let whoever is in charge know right away.

2. Have someone help you "take a balance."

That means having a friend sit near the back of the room and signal to you if you should speak closer, farther away, more directly, more loudly or softly. He or she should also let you know just how clearly the sound system carries your voice.

Many speakers, especially beginners, feel that getting someone to help with these checks is big-dealing, role-playing, overdoing the speech. It all depends on how important your speech is to you. If you want to be absolutely sure of having everything possible help you give an effective speech, you won't be concerned about having someone help you. If you're going to give a one-minute announcement about next week's meeting, taking a balance and other checks are of course not usually worthwhile.

Experienced speakers, when they have someone help them take a balance, almost always do so before the audience gathers.

Some people suggest having someone in the audience to signal to let you know how you sound while you're actually giving your speech. I find that very distracting. A few times I've had my wife out there in the audience to cue me. Often I forget to look at her. The few times I've finally spotted her I was already well into my speech. Besides, I'd then have trouble remembering the meaning of the signals we'd set up—did that tug on her ear mean I'm doing great, or that I should speak louder, get closer to the mike, or buy her a set of earrings?

3. Practice raising and lowering the mike.

If you're short, chances are the guy who speaks just before you is tall. Or, the chairman may tell you before the program starts, "Just set the mike at whatever height you need, and we'll leave it there." Then someone shows up to make just a brief announcement and moves your carefully set mike into a totally different position.

"But raising or lowering a mike can't be a problem!" the novice will say. "Why practice? All you do is pull it up or push it down—don't you?"

Sometimes!

Some mike stands have little buttons—often hidden on the other side from where the speaker's facing—which have to be pushed in before the mike will move. Other mikes are moved by first twisting some type of locking mechanism. Others have no lock system at all —you just have to push or pull, sometimes with the strength of Mr. America.

4. Find out if someone is to control the sound system.

Often a custodian sets up the public address system, turns it on, sets it at the volume that worked last week, and goes off to sweep out the library. And generally, the older, weaker, less reliable the sound system, the harder that guy is to find.

Of course some sound systems are run by skilled technicians. Usually they are perfectionists. They'll ask *you* to check the mike and to take a balance. They may also ask such questions as, "Would you like a bit more reverberation? How are the lower ranges—suit your voice OK?"

Few speakers know the answers to such questions. And the technician knows you don't know. I just tell them, "Do whatever you think best to make me sound *great!*"

When there is a technician present—an authentic, qualified technician—the sound system is virtually always perfect. The mike goes up and down easily. You can move away from being right in front of the mike and that technician will adjust his rows of knobs to keep your voice coming through. And when there's a technician around the system *never* breaks down. Well, almost never.

There's a logical reason for such reliability: Most technicians take pride in their equipment. They want it to work, to make themselves look good. And clearly, an auditorium that bothers to have a technician present is run by someone who also has pride in providing quality facilities.

The problems come when there is no technician. And that's much more usually the case. Sometimes the chairman runs the sound system. Sometimes a member of the organization handles it. Usually he does it for every meeting of the group, so he probably knows what he's doing. On the other hand, I've even had a chairman tell me, "Say—if you want to use a mike, you'll have to turn on and adjust the equipment yourself."

Again, you're on the spot. How should you handle a do-it-yourself arrangement?

First, take a fast look at the equipment. Decide if you want to try to fiddle with all those controls. If not, say to the chairman, "You must have more experience with this gear than I have —can you set it for me, please?" And walk away. Usually, he'll take over.

Or, take another look at the size of the audience and the room in which you're speaking. Perhaps you'll do better—be safer—to just speak up, give your talk without using the sound system.

5. Learn how to turn the sound OFF!

At the very least, *always* look at *every* sound system you're to use and find the switch marked "OFF." Then, no matter who's running the thing—bumbling beginner or trained technician—you can take over and turn the equipment off when it's not operating as it should. And that happens more times than Marconi, Edison, and all those other great inventors imagined!

Because:

6. Remember: Once a sound system starts acting up, you're in trouble!

A sound system will not *once* make sounds on its own —distort your voice, squeal, or otherwise distract. "Not *once*"—but repeatedly!!

Once the mike starts to cut on and off, chances are high it will continue to do so. If a system howls once, it will usually do so again and again.

Here's what you—as a speaker—should do.

First time the sound system acts up, stop speaking. Look around. Hope that custodian or technician will take action. The distraction may disappear in just a few seconds.

Then go on with your speech.

If the sound system misbehaves again, stop speaking again. Give the chairman a real look—one that lets him know you want him to solve the problem—now! Consider asking him to get it fixed.

When the system's working again, continue your speech.

But if the sound system acts up again—a third time— leave it!

Whether it's feedback (howling), clicking, cutting in-and-out, suddenly becoming too loud or too quiet, whatever—three interruptions are enough!

Ask that technician, or custodian, or chairman to turn the thing off. Or, go turn it off yourself!

Then just continue your speech without using the mike.

You can set it aside, or move away from the lectern.

And speak up. Do your best to be heard. Speak louder—but don't yell at your listeners.

If you can't be heard by most, you'd just as well quit speaking entirely. To continue putting up with a sound system that's not working properly is a waste of your time. And your listeners'. There's no point in all of you having to put up with a bothersome sound system. You'll have little likelihood of attaining your purpose in speaking while the sound system is fooling around. So just stop talking!

7. Avoid making unpleasant sounds over the mike.

A cough will come over many mikes sounding like an earthquake. A sneeze will sound like the blow-in of an oil well. The rustle of paper close to a microphone is used on both radio and television programs to make the sound of a fire. Crunch cellophane near a mike and you have the sound of a major forest fire.

So, be careful. If you bang on the lectern to emphasize a point, the mike may pick up the sound and really startle your listeners. If you're a nervous finger-tapper, listen to find out if your audience is hearing that as a drum corps practicing for the next parade.

8. Don't say ANYTHING confidential near a mike.

During my years as a radio announcer, then later as a TV producer, there's one story I'd heard told about a network anchorman and a well-known sportscaster. And just about everyone in broadcasting has heard this same classic story.

An announcer is reading the funny papers on the air for a kids' show. He finishes, thinks his mike is "off," and says to a friend visiting the studio, "That will hold the little bastards for another day!"

Of course his mike was still "on." All those sweet little kiddies—and their parents—were properly shocked.

That story has been told so often I wonder if it's true. But I did watch former President Nixon make a similar flub. It was during one of his campaign speeches which was telecast nationwide. He was nearing the end of his talk. Someone just off-camera caught his eye. Nixon looked. Then a slight wave of concern swept his face. He looked at his notes, concluded his speech in a few brief sentences. Just as he finished you could hear someone say, "NO!—No—you've got one *more* minute!" Now the audience was applauding. Nixon could no longer continue speaking. He smiled his usual broad grin. But from between his clenched teeth I clearly heard him say, "Who in the hell gave me that signal?"

Mikes are dangerous. Say something you want just one person to hear, and a mike will, it seems, suddenly blossom out with an exceptionally sensitive ability to pick up your words.

Watch the telecasts of the national political conventions. Almost every evening, sometimes more often, you can spot a speaker saying something confidential to another person on the platform—and the remark ends up being broadcast all over America.

Don't let yourself be caught in such a situation—even if it's in front of just a handful of your fellow workers at a company conference. Always consider every mike to be "on" all the time.

9. Don't be the "great voice" that doesn't need a mike.

You've probably heard such speakers. They stride up to the speaker's platform with the authority of a general leading a charge. Their macho presence fills the hall. Dramatically, with scorn, they set the mike aside. "Don't need that thing—you'll hear me fine!"

Then they spend an hour or so yelling at you. They speak with no shadings. Their most casual comments and their most significant statements all come out like the roar of a jet. After hearing such speeches, you—as a listener—are tired. More important, it's hard for you to remember, often, the major points. Everything came out with too much volume, too much emphasis, too little selectivity.

Such speakers have not yet learned the very valuable assistance they could get from a mike—if they'd only learn how to use one.

As stated early in this chapter, a mike can let you talk conversationally, personably, individually with every member of your audience. No matter how many people are present, you can make each one feel you're talking on a one-to-one basis—if you use the microphone effectively.

CHECKPOINTS:
USING A MICROPHONE

When you're about to go give a speech, review the following points to help insure you'll use the sound system properly.

_____ 1. Check the microphone ahead of time.
_____ 2. Have someone help you take a balance.
_____ 3. Practice raising and lowering the mike.
_____ 4. Find out if someone is to control the sound system.
_____ 5. Learn how to turn the sound OFF!
_____ 6. Remember: Once a sound system starts acting up, you're in trouble!
_____ 7. Avoid making unpleasant sounds over the mike.
_____ 8. Don't say ANYTHING confidential near a mike!
_____ 9. Don't be the great voice that doesn't need a mike!

19

Answering Questions

*It is a thing of no great
difficulty to raise objections
against another man's oration
—nay, a very easy matter; but
to produce a better in its
place is a work extremely
troublesome.*

PLUTARCH

MOMENTS AGO YOU concluded your speech. The applause was loud and long. Now hands are waving as many listeners respond to your invitation to ask questions.

After all the work of preparing and presenting a speech, answering questions should be easy. But almost every day you can tune in to TV news programs presenting fine examples of how *not* to answer questions—unless you want to mislead, avoid, confuse. For example:

* On a network newscast, you can watch a sly senator twist questions to new meanings.
* On a local program, you can catch a crafty candidate seem to say yes as he really says no.
* On another station, a wily bureaucrat will chew up limited air time with long-winded replies which say nothing—filling time so he won't have to answer more than a few questions.

237

Answering questions effectively is easy if you follow these twelve techniques.

1. Listen carefully to the question.

Try to catch the *intent* as well as the content of what is asked. This is a critical point. Not all questions are asking what they seem to ask.

Assume you've just given a speech about solar energy. A likely question from someone in your audience might be, "How do you think they'll get the money for the research that's needed?" That question seems to be clear-cut; it's merely seeking your opinion. But suppose the question comes from the president of the local tax-payers' association. Then the *intent* of the question might be, "Won't it take more taxes to pay for the research?"

You might answer, "Such research is a very big job; we'll need a major effort by our government." But then you'll probably lose that taxpayer as a supporter of your proposal. You could say, "Such research is a very big job; we'll need a major effort by our government—perhaps paid for by reducing research on space, for one thing, for a few years, so our taxes will not have to be raised." That answer may keep your questioner supporting your idea. So one way to figure out the intent of a question is to know your audience.

Another way is to be alert for certain key words or phrases in a question. One person may ask, "Do you really think that? . . ." Such wording may really mean, "Oh come now, you don't seriously think that, . . . do you???" Other questions which may signal meanings other than their actual wordings are: "Isn't it about time to . . . ?" and "You mean to try to tell us that . . . ?"

Finally, the inflection or emphasis a questioner places on particular words may also tell you he's asking you something with a hidden meaning. The question, "How can they do that?" can be spoken with a calm, even voice. Then it would sound like a simple request for information. But those same words can mean doubt or disagreement if stated with this emphasis: "How *CAN* they do that?"

2. Repeat the question.

That will help everyone in the audience to hear the question. And it will help you be sure you heard the question correctly. Answer a question which is different from the one which was asked and you'll probably get many unhappy listeners.

You have probably been a member of an audience when this guide to answering questions was ignored. The questioner, usually seated in the front rows, close to the speaker, asks a question in a voice loud enough to just reach the speaker. The many listeners in the rear of the room hear just a mumble. The speaker starts to answer, without first repeating the question as he should. He gets partway through an answer only to be interrupted by a harsh shout from someone in the back of the room—"Couldn't hear the question! Please repeat it!!" That's distracting to the speaker because it interferes with his flow of ideas as he's trying to state the answer. It bothers the audience, too, as their listening is also interrupted.

If there is a chairman, he should accept the questions from the audience, repeat them, then step aside to let the speaker answer them. If there is no chairman, the speaker should repeat the questions himself.

3. Define terms.

This will help insure that you—and your audience— are considering the same point.

A classic example of the need to define terms occurred repeatedly during our nation's considerations of amnesty for draft dodgers of the Vietnam War. Time and again a Washington official would say, "I'm for amnesty. Let the draft dodgers back in our country, give them the opoprtunity to pay their fines and serve their time in jail, and then we can forgive and forget their running away." But that's not what "amnesty" means. My dictionary says it is a "pardon granted to a large group of individuals," and "pardon" means "the excusing of an offense without exacting a penalty."

If those speakers had defined "amnesty," they would have saved a lot of time and confusion. If you'll define the terms you use as you answer questions following your speeches, your replies will be clearer and more likely to be accepted by your listeners.

4. Divide a question which has several parts.

Many people will ask one long question which really includes several different questions. It's not unusual for someone to string a stack of questions into one long rambling query, like this:

If your plan is put into effect—and I was wondering if you thought it really would work, and when we might expect it to start—wouldn't it put some people out of work, and how do you think they should be helped?

That's really four questions in one. Try to answer that in one big reply and you'll probably confuse many of your listeners.

But break that question into its subquestions, answer each one in turn, and your replies should be much clearer and therefore more likely to be accepted.

For example, you could answer the questioner just quoted by saying:

You're really asking several questions. First, you ask if I think my plan would really work. I do indeed, because I've seen it work in other plants which are very much like ours. Then you ask when we might start. If we approve the plan at this meeting, it could begin within three months. You also ask if the plan would put some people out of work. No, because sales would increase, so we'll keep all those people turning out many more units. Finally, you ask how we'll help those people. We'll set up a training program, and in two weeks they'll know how to operate the new equipment proposed in this plan.

5. If asked for facts, present them as directly and briefly as possible.

You as a listener may have reacted negatively to speakers you've heard who fail to answer questions directly. Someone may ask, "Just how high is our accident rate?" The speaker replies, "Well, let's look at the record. Ten years ago . . ." and he's off on a long history of the rate of accidents. Instead, he should get right to the point—"The accident rate is now twenty-two per month."

If you, as the speaker answering questions, feel that a further explanation is needed, give it *after* you've presented the information you were asked for. Still, you should be brief and get on to the next questioner promptly.

6. If asked for an opinion, give it, then support it with evidence.

Suppose you're asked, "Do you think our safety record is good enough?" Your reply should start with either a yes or a no. *Don't* reply as you've heard so many speakers do, wandering around in words such as:

Well, of course no safety record is ever 'good enough,' as long as just one person is hurt. And I think we should improve our standards, but we have been trying. It would cost a lot of money to improve safety, and I'm not saying I'd recommend that right now . . .

On and on go some speakers. Answers should be brief, specific, direct. Don't give rambling, conflicting, confusing explanations leading up to your answer. And don't follow a fact with a wandering, detailed explanation.

7. Relate your answers to your main speech.

Sometimes a questioner didn't understand a point in your speech. He asks you for more details. You should restate your point, briefly.

But there's a real danger in how you word your reply. It may sound like a put-down if you answer, "Well, I covered that in my speech. Like I said then . . ." To some in your audience, that may sound like you are really saying, "Stupid—I already told you!" So when a question relates directly to something you already said in your speech, restate it but don't emphasize that you are repeating your point. Rather, state the point in different words. If possible, try to present additional—different—data to support your idea. Alternate wording of a point may win over to your view some listeners who did not accept your first version.

8. If a question is strongly argumentative— answer it directly, maintaining your view.

Try to avoid arguments with a questioner. Rarely does a subject of any importance have just one solution, one viewpoint. You might point out that while the question has merit, you happen to believe otherwise. You then might add an example or other data. Don't feel because one or a few in your audience ask argumentative questions you've lost all your listeners. The argumentative questioners may well be representative of but a small minority of your listeners.

Furthermore, an argumentative questioner may be just trying to draw out more information. Milton wrote:

Where there is much desire to learn, there of necessity will be much arguing, much writing, many opinions; for opinion in good men is but knowledge in the making.

9. *If you don't know the answer, say so!*

Nearly 100 years ago Mark Twain wrote: "I was gratified to be able to answer promptly, and I did. I said I didn't know."

Another good reply when you don't know the answer: Refer the questioner to some place he might find the answer—a book, study, expert, or some other likely source for the information.

Finally, you might offer to find the information for the questioner. You could say: "I'm sorry, I really don't know the answer to that. But if you'll write your question on a slip of paper, along with your address and phone number, I'll find out and get back to you."

That reply has several advantages. Many of your listeners will be impressed by both your frankness and your offer to assist. It makes you sound open and honest. It tends to cut off other questions on that same subject. And chances are you won't have to look up the answer anyway—few questioners will bother to take the time and effort to give you the question in writing.

10. *Call on as many different people in your audience as possible.*

That is, avoid letting one person, or a few, monopolize your question-and-answer period. To the first person who tries to ask a second question, say something like: "Let's hear the questions of other people in our audience first—and I'll try to save time to get back to you for another question later, after everyone else has had a turn."

If you say something like that early and firmly, you'll set a standard for other questioners to follow.

11. *Don't let a questioner give a speech.*

This may be a difficult problem to handle tactfully. If you interrupt the questioner, some of your listeners may think you're unfairly cutting off a question. If you let a long-winded questioner go on, others in your audience may feel you're letting one listener take over. And certainly the questioner will not like being cut short.

Still, you will probably have about as many listeners who agree with your action as those who don't. Sometimes you simply must be authoritative. Interrupt and ask briefly but pointedly, "What is your question, please?"

12. *If someone has difficulty wording a question, assist.*

Sometimes a courteous "I think I understand your question" will solve this problem. Other times you just have to let the individual struggle along expressing his fuzzy thinking as best he can, even though he is chewing up your time and your listeners' patience.

But sometimes those hard-to-phrase questions are sound and relevant. If you cut a questioner off too soon, you will probably make her unhappy, and others in your audience may also feel you should have let the person state the question in her own way. Even a nod of agreement from you, or a gesture, before the questioner has finished, may turn her off and also displease some of your listeners.

To help such questioners, you might say something such as: "May I help you word your question?—Are you asking . . . ?"

If the audience is small and especially friendly with each other, you might also ask someone else in the audience to help word the question. You might say, "I think I know what you're asking—but would someone else also like to try to pose that question, so I'll be sure?"

Now you have a dozen techniques to help you answer questions following your speeches. In essence, your goal in answering questions is to get every member of your audience—whether they asked a question or not—to think about you just what British author Kenneth Grahame wrote in 1895: "I began to like this man. He answered your questions briefly and to the point."

CHECKPOINTS:
ANSWERING QUESTIONS

Check off each item as you prepare to give a speech after which you might have to answer questions.

_____ 1. Listen carefully to the question.

_____ 2. Repeat the question.

_____ 3. Define terms.

_____ 4. Divide a question which has several parts.

_____ 5. If asked for facts, present them as directly and briefly as possible.

_____ 6. If asked for an opinion, give it, then support it with data.

_____ 7. Relate your answers to your main speech.

_____ 8. If a question is strongly argumentative, answer it directly, maintaining your view.

_____ 9. If you don't know the answer, say so.

_____ 10. Call on as many different people in your audience as possible.

_____ 11. Don't let a questioner give a speech.

_____ 12. If someone has difficulty wording a question, assist.

20

Dealing with Distractions

A man's character is revealed by his speech.

MENANDER

JUST AS YOU'RE about to start your after-dinner speech, a waiter drops a full tray of dishes.

You're at the climax of your speech and the lights go out.

A plane buzzes the auditorium. Screeching tires announce a drag race in the adjacent parking lot. A fight breaks out in the next room.

The sound system goes dead. Worse—the sound system starts to hum, howl, click, detract.

Or a heckler yells at you. Well, at least you're now involved in a problem faced by some of the world's most famous speakers!

When President Reagan was interrupted while speaking to a group of congressional candidates, he yelled at the heckler, "Shut up!"

When presidential candidate George McGovern was repeatedly interrupted by a heckler in Battle Creek, Michigan, he yelled at the detractor, "Kiss my ass!"

When Senator S. I. Hayakawa was president of San Francisco State University, he stopped students who were interrupting one of his speeches by pulling the wires out of their public address system.

Such replies may not be your style. Still, the high ratings of some television shows seems to say that many viewers admire or are intrigued by both hecklers and the put-down of hecklers. For years the "Dean Martin Celebrity Roast" had a huge audience. His show consisted of about a dozen stars heckling a celebrity for about fifty-five-minutes—minus commercials—followed by the recipient giving a five-minute reply to his or her tormentors.

That TV show started a fashion in speaking. Local clubs all over America began holding roasts. A Chamber of Commerce, for example, would roast the mayor by having the town druggist, high-school principal, car dealer, and other community folks fire insults. Indeed, several writers made money by marketing ready-made insults for such hometown roasts.

Apparently many of us have a vision of ourselves as "heckler-killers." We may dream of being able to deliver the fast comeback as if we were:

Johnny Carson—A heckle from someone in his studio audience will bring Johnny to a sudden stop; a smirk will twist across his face and he'll give a line such as 'May a sick camel leave his tidings on your best suit!'

Don Rickles—talk back to him and he'll give you a penetrating stare and growl, 'I'm going to keep my eye on you!'

Milton Berle—interrupt him and he'll often snarl, 'Wat-za-matta—your brother an only child?'

Jack Carter—heckle him and he'll look you in the eye and ask, 'Why don't you be content with what you are? Nothing!!'

But most of us realize those cutting remarks come from a stable of writers and years of practice.

However, hecklers are not the only distractions a

speaker might face. There may be a crying baby. He may start other tots crying. Then, a couple of people can start whispering and soon they'll get so loud they interrupt your thinking. And if one person ducks out for a comfort run, many others often get the urge. More frequently, a speaker will face a cougher; just one cough can set off a wave of hacking throughout an audience!

Most distractions usually remain minor. The parents of that crying youngster are usually doing what they can to bring quiet for your speech. Whisperers are aften hushed by listeners sitting nearby. That parade to the john usually slows—finally. Coughers usually, eventually, find their cough drops and settle down.

But what if you do have to take action? To get a crying youngster quieted, try a pause. If the crying continues, take another pause plus a warning look at the parents. That usually works. You might silence those whispers by giving the same treatment. If they continue, look at the chairman, then nod toward the distracters.

Consider the possibility that those coughers and the people streaming to the rest rooms just might be right —perhaps it is time for a pause in the program. People need a break from speeches after an hour or so of listening. If you're introduced to give a speech after the audience has been hearing other speakers for nearly an hour, your speech will be more successful if you give the audience, say, a ten-minute rest period before you begin. Even if you have to take the time from your own speaking period, a break after several speeches will almost always improve the attention listeners give you.

But what about hecklers? The fact is, they're rare indeed.

When was the last time you heard a heckler in person? Mostly, hecklers are more in the nightmares of speakers than in the real-life world. Hecklers just seem much more numerous because they show up on television newscasts so vividly. They are the newsperson's salvation from the routine reporting of routine speeches. In a lifetime of speaking, most speakers never face a heckler.

Still, speakers wonder, Just how should I deal with a distraction?

There are six clear-cut steps for solving such problems.

1. Pause.

This is effective for several reasons. First, it's obviously the natural thing to do. You don't have to do any thinking—just do what comes naturally.

As you pause, think through what you really heard. Did the heckler, for example, sound serious? Or drunk? Did he sound like he was starting a major disagreement with you? Or did it sound like a brief, hopefully one-time interruption? Your answer can help you decide what to do next.

But pauses are difficult for many speakers, especially when facing a distracter. Some speakers want to rush on with what they've got to say. That's what many of us do in conversation when we're interrupted. It's much like the typical schoolteacher's reaction to a noisy class. The teacher will usually speak faster and louder. He'll try to drown out the talking students with more words and more volume.

But have you ever seen a professional speaker facing a noisy audience? He does just the opposite. He'll speak slower. He'll lower the volume of his voice. Stage actors do that for the traditionally noisy audiences at Wednesday matinees. Lecturers will drop to a whisper so their listeners have to quiet down to hear. Politicians—knowledgeable ones—facing a barrage of questions from a team of reporters will speak slowly and quietly. President Reagan uses that technique. California's Governor Brown hasn't learned it yet. Faced with persistent questioners, he lets his voice get shrill, loud, excited; that simply increases the fire of his distracters.

There's another advantage to the pause. It lets your audience know that you've noted the distraction. And the pause can give your listeners time to figure out what *their* reaction—if any—might be. Some in the audience may hush, hiss, boo, or answer the heckler for you.

If they do, you should be able to go on with your speech. Furthermore, you now have at least some of your listeners clearly on your side. That's good, of course, because other listeners who may have also mentally objected to the heckler but were not moved to react openly, may now have had their feelings reinforced to support you.

But if the pause doesn't work and you're interrupted again, then:

2. Acknowledge the distracter.

In a quiet, assured, authoritative tone, say something such as:

You may be right.

Some people do have that view.

That may be true, but let me present to you the reasons why I believe as I do.

Then, continue to pause. Make it a good, long, significant pause. That will give you time to collect your thoughts and prepare yourself for staying calm. This pause also gives the heckler time to decide if he or she is going to continue to interrupt you. And the pause gives your listeners another chance to decide if they are going to help you quiet the heckler.

If the heckler replies to your brief acknowledgment, or if the heckling continues, then:

3. Offer to talk with the heckler later.

You might say:

How about you and I talking about your views after my speech?

That's an interesting point. Could you tell me more about it after my speech?

To some hecklers and some members of an audience such a statement will appear to be a generous, brave, fair offer. But others may view the same situation and consider your invitation a cop-out—a slick attempt to avoid a confrontation, a ducking of a difference of opinion.

In many situations, the offer to meet later will silence the heckler. But a hot and heavy heckler may reply with something such as, "You afraid to talk about my view now?"

Again, your best defense is another pause. That will give your listeners time to decide to react, if they are ever going to. By now the lines of agreeing or objecting to you will probably be set.

If you're still alone—if no one in the audience has spoken up for you, if no one has tried to help you quiet the heckler, then:

4. Invite the heckler to come on up and speak.

For a persistent heckler, you might just as well give him the spotlight. If you continue to try to talk as he continues to heckle, you're just dividing the attention of your listeners. Neither you nor the heckler is likely to be heard clearly, completely.

Try saying something such as:

Would you like to come on up here and speak from this rostrum, so everyone here can hear you better?

Tell you what, friend, you go ahead and speak. I won't interrupt you. Then you let me give my speech, and you don't interrupt me. Fair enough?

Your heckler now has three options. He can shut up. Great!—problem solved!

Or, he or she can accept your invitation and come up

to speak. If he does that, it's likely that he's not at all as prepared and polished a speaker as you are. Chances are high that he'll fumble words, twist ideas, confuse his thinking—his adrenalin is probably pumping up his nerves. So when you do get your turn to continue with your speech, your views should come out clearer, more specific, more memorable than the heckler's. You should end up by presenting the stronger, more effective speech.

The heckler's third option—the worst possible situation—is that he'll keep on heckling you. But by now, certainly, your audience must be turning against him. You've been fair. You've been calm. You've invited him to speak and he's now shown he really just wants to interrupt. Now it's time to:

5. Let your audience assume responsibility for quieting the heckler.

Another pause, along with an appealing look around your audience should motivate at least a few listeners to try silencing the distracter. Some may call out, "Quiet! Let the speaker speak!!" Or the ultimate to the heckler, "Throw him out!!!"

After all, your listeners are present to hear you, not the heckler. A heckler interrupts the listeners every bit as much as the speaker. The audience will generally recognize that and take action.

And if they don't?

6. Ask the chairperson to solve the problem.

Of course, the chairperson should have taken over by now anyway. But if he or she hasn't, just turn to whoever introduced you, or whoever is running the meeting, and say something such as, "Would you please help out here?"

A few groups have a sergeant-at-arms who should move in to help you.

Note the basic concept behind all six of these techniques: *The speaker should avoid becoming engaged in an argument with a heckler*. That just gets you, the speaker, all worked up, usually ends up in a shouting match. Certainly such an argument does not help you achieve the purpose of your speech.

It's a good idea to keep in mind these effective techniques for dealing with distractions. But don't keep thinking about the distracters you might face. Don't keep worrying about a heckler throwing verbal barbs at you. Remember: *Hecklers are rare indeed*.

The problem is, in essence, that historians enjoy pointing to the great hecklers and the great put-down of hecklers.

There was that day in the British Parliament when Nancy Astor, the first woman elected to that body, interrupted a speech by Winston Churchill. She said, "Winston, if you were my husband, I would flavor your coffee with poison!" Churchill's reply: "Madam, if I were your husband, I should drink it!"

And California Governor Earl Warren, speaking to an audience much larger than he'd expected, said, "I'm pleased to see such a dense crowd here tonight." A heckler roared back, "We ain't all dense!"

CHECKPOINTS:
DEALING WITH DISTRACTIONS

Occasionally—especially if you think you might meet some distractions when you give a speech—go through the following checklist to refresh your memory of how to handle such situations.

_____ 1. Distractions are rare.
_____ 2. Most distractions are minor.
_____ 3. Most will solve themselves:
      _____ (1) Crying babies are usually quieted by their parents.
      _____ (2) Whisperers usually tire or are silenced by nearby listeners.
      _____ (3) Rest room trips finally slow, stop.
      _____ (4) Coughers usually get control of themselves.
_____ 4. If the meeting has been going for an hour or so, consider giving the audience a short break.
_____ 5. Handling a heckler:
      _____ (1) Pause.
      _____ (2) Acknowledge.
      _____ (3) Offer to talk with the heckler later.
      _____ (4) Invite the heckler to come up to speak.
      _____ (5) Let your audience assume responsibility for quieting the heckler.
      _____ (6) Ask chairperson to solve the problem.
_____ 6. There's no point continuing with distractions.
_____ 7. Avoid arguing.
_____ 8. Key point: Don't worry!—hecklers are rare!

21

"... And so,
in Conclusion ..."

> *Speech is civilization itself.
> The word, even the most
> contradictory word, preserves
> contact—it is silence which
> isolates.*
>
> **THOMAS MANN**

LET ME SUMMARIZE the basic point of *How to Speak Like a Pro.*

First, *relax.*

Sure, that's easy to say, hard to do. Giving a speech scares most of us. Even professional speakers. A former paratrooper, a student in one of my speech classes, told me, "Giving a speech is like jumping out of a plane—when the chute doesn't open!" He'd done that. But he had a second chute—his backup. This book can be your backup when you speak.

Next, *be yourself.*

Don't try to sound like any of those golden-voiced spellbinders you see on TV or hear at conventions. None of them can speak in your style, express your ideas, as well as you can in your own personal, individual way. Be "the unique you" which today's pop-psychologists emphasize.

Third, *prepare your speeches.*

Follow the eight steps to successful speaking which

257

are detailed in this book. Use the nineteen lists of checkpoints. They'll help insure you're thoroughly prepared for every speech you'll likely give, and ready for almost any speaking problem you might face. The founder of the Boy Scouts, Lord Baden–Powell, gave those kids a motto that fits public speaking perfectly: **Be prepared.**

As a final insurance to help you prepare your speeches quickly, easily, there's a checklist on the next page that brings all the basic steps together. Use it as its name says—as "The Basic Checklist for Speaking." When you need more help in any of the "8 Steps to Successful Speaking," read the instructions for those steps as presented earlier in this book. If you need help with any of "The 4 Key Details to Smooth Speaking," review the tips for each as offered in the last chapters of this book.

BUT REMEMBER: *use the checklists as you prepare.* Don't get up before an audience hoping that the right techniques and the perfect words will flash into your mind right them. To speak like a pro, do what the pros do—*prepare!*

CHECKPOINTS:
THE BASIC CHECKLIST FOR SPEAKING

As you prepare your speeches, check off each of the following points. FOR DETAILS ABOUT EACH POINT, SEE THE PREVIOUS CHAPTERS IN THIS BOOK.

The 8 Steps to Successful Speaking:

_____ 1. Control your stage fright.

_____ 2. Select your subject.

_____ 3. Gather your ideas and information.

_____ 4. Organize your material.

_____ 5. Plan the beginning of your speech.

_____ 6. Plan the ending of your speech.

_____ 7. Practice your speech.

_____ 8. Present your speech.

The 4 Key Details to Smooth Speaking:

_____ 1. Check arrangements.

_____ 2. Know how to use a microphone.

_____ 3. Be prepared to answer questions.

_____ 4. Know how to deal with distractions.

Now, in closing, I must give you two warnings.

First, you should consider the tips and techniques in this book as guides, not laws. There are very few hard-and-fast rules to effective speaking. Speech is an art. Speech is creative. This book presents techniques which most speakers find most effective for most speaking situations. But often the truly successful speaker is one who masters these guides, then changes them a bit to meet his or her own personality, and thereby becomes still more effective.

The other warning: *You just might get hooked on speaking!*

Speaking is indeed addictive for many people. You can get a real high from the flow of communication through public speaking. There's excitement in the audience–speaker relationship. Once you've heard laughs for your jokes and applause for your ideas, then you just might want to—*have* to!—go on speaking. Some three-and-a-half centuries ago English poet Ben Jonson wrote:

Whom the disease of talking once possesseth, he can never hold his peace. Nay, rather than he will not discourse, he will hire men to hear him.

What should you do if the thrill of speaking in public captures you?

You can volunteer. Many good causes need speakers. Conservation. Self-help projects. Fund drives. Youth groups. Political organizations. Churches. Clubs. Community programs. Reform efforts of all kinds. The list could go on and on.

And you can continue to improve your speaking skills. Courses, seminars, and training sessions are offered by many community colleges, four-year colleges and universities, adult schools, and other institutions.

Another possibility: Consider joining *Toastmasters,* the worldwide organization in which members help each other become better speakers. More than two million people have benefited from its "Success/Leadership Programs." Besides training in various types and levels of speaking, *Toastmasters* conducts workshops in related skills—listening, conducting meetings, parliamentary procedure, and such. For more information, get in touch with a local club. There's probably one close to wherever you live or work—more than 5,000 in every state and forty-seven foreign countries. Or consider *Toastmistresses,* a separate organization with about 1,500 clubs. Both groups include men and women.

Now, as you think about your future in public speaking, these words by Scottish author Robert Louis Stevenson may be of help:

The first duty of man is to speak; that is his chief business in the world.

About the Author

LEON FLETCHER has taught public speaking to adult classes, community college students and high school students for over 25 years. He is the author of one of the most popular college textbooks on speech, HOW TO DESIGN & DELIVER A SPEECH (Harper & Row), and has written and produced programs for educational television and instructional materials for RCA, Standard Oil, McGraw-Hill and the California Department of Education, among others. Mr. Fletcher lives in Monterey, California.